SLE

4

THEATRES, SPACES, ENVIRONMENTS: EIGHTEEN PROJECTS

Brooks McNamara

Jerry Rojo

Richard Schechner

THEATRES, SPACES, ENVIRONMENTS:

EIGHTEEN PROJECTS

Brooks McNamara
Jerry Rojo
Richard Schechner

Drama Book Specialists (Publishers)
New York

All rights reserved under the International and Pan American Copyright Conventions. For information address Drama Book Specialists (Publishers), 150 West 52nd Street, New York, New York 10019.

Library of Congress Cataloging in Publication Data

McNamara, Brooks.
    Theatres, spaces, environments.

    1. Theaters—United States—Stage-setting and scenery. 2. Theaters—United States—Construction. I. Rojo, Jerry. II. Schechner, Richard, 1934- III. Title.
PN2091.S8M24   792   75-29018
ISBN 0-910482-63-2

Printed in the United States of America

To our Parents

Margaret McNamara
Elmer McNamara

Dorothy Rojo
Guadalupe Rojo

Selma Schechner
Sheridan Schechner

Acknowledgments & Thanks

In many different ways people have helped us conceive, build and use these spaces. Sometimes. an administrator made it possible for us to work; often a performer came up with an idea that made the space better; just as often a craftsman added his own touch to a project and improved it.

We want to thank The Performance Group, The Manhattan Project, Section Ten, the New York University School of the Arts, the University of Connecticut Department of Dramatic Arts, the University of British Columbia Theatre Department and the State University of New York at New Paltz.

Money for projects came not only from buyers but from endowments and foundations, and we thank the National Endowment for the Arts, the New York State Council on the Arts, the Ford Foundation, the Rockefeller Foundation, the JDR 3rd Fund, the Shubert Foundation.

Many individuals have helped us with these projects and with putting together this book. We thank Ellen LeCompte, Rickel Twersky, Maurice McCellen, Robert Adzema, Ed Madden, Marty Kapell, James Clayburgh, Ronald Fenn, George Yourke, Barry Klein, David Heilweil, Norman Young, David Oppenheim, Michael Miller, Edmund Seagrave, Richard Brown and John Herr.

Finally, as Professor J. S. Rothbard reminds us, "it's not the book that counts but its readers." We expect everyone we've thanked to read our book.

B. Mc.
J. R.
R. S.

Contents

Foreword

**Brooks McNamara
Jerry Rojo
Richard Schechner**

In 1971 the authors, along with Edmund Seagrave and Jerry Powell, formed Environmental Theatre Associates. The new corporation was not set up just to design environments but to create a wide variety of spaces for performances. For our business cards we chose the words "theatres, spaces, environments" as most accurately describing the range of projects we were prepared to undertake.

We've borrowed these same three words for the title of this book, and wish the book more commercial success than its namesake. We think the eighteen projects described in our book are different but related. Present is the same impulse to negotiate with all the space in which a performance takes place, including the spaces usually reserved for spectators, the areas where rehearsals are conducted, the shop where scenery is built, the offices where business is transacted, and so on. Negotiation also implies that as a process unfolds it will change—so that the relationship between drawings, models, construction, and finished space is not one in which each successive step translates the former steps, but an evolutionary process in which change is not only possible but inevitable and welcome. Our notion of process is only apparently new, it is at least as old as the construction of medieval cathedrals. All of the projects described involve Jerry Rojo. Brooks McNamara and Richard Schechner were involved in some of them. We join together to do a book because our community of interest and scholarship make us the best choice to mull over the problems involved. The work included in this book is clearly influenced by that style of performance called "environmental theatre." Further, the work described in this book has decisively shaped environmental theatre. Rather than define environmental in this foreword, we leave the book and its projects to speak their own languages.

Theatres, Spaces, Environments is organized around three basic types of construction for performance. In Part I we describe nine projects, each of which transforms an existing space, generally by creating within it a "fixed" (permanent) theatre or performance space. Part II records five temporary environments constructed in the same space, The Performing Garage in New York City. The Garage is the theatre of The Performance Group, founded by Richard Schechner. In Part III we describe four examples of environments built in widely differing spaces.

In discussing each of these projects we've tried to provide through text, photographs, and drawings a clear account of the work, as well as some of the theory underlying it. We prepared the book by meeting, looking at photos and drawings, and tape-recording our conversations. We've known each other for nearly ten years now, so this method of informal talk got us deeply into our subject. It also allowed for actual dialogue. Needless to say the tapes have been edited.

A basis for understanding the work discussed here has been provided by Schechner in *Environmental Theater*:

> The environmentalist is not trying to create the illusion of a place; he wants to create a functioning space. This space will be used by many different kinds of people, not only the performers. The stage designer is often concerned with effect: how does it *look* from the house? The environmentalist is concerned with structure and use: how does it *work*? Often the stage designer's set is used from a distance—don't touch this, don't stand on that—but everything the environmentalist builds must work. Stage designing is two-dimensional, a kind of propped-up painting. Environmental design is strictly three-dimensional. If it's there, it's got to work.

This book is here. We want it to work.

1

Brooks McNamara

The Environmental Tradition

In 1967 a group of performers, assembled by Richard Schechner, Franklin Adams, and Paul Epstein produced a unique version of Eugene Ionesco's *Victims of Duty* at the studio theatre of Le Petit Théâtre du Vieux Carré in the French Quarter of New Orleans. The New Orleans Group moved out the seats that usually filled the room and moved in a huge pile of platforms, flats, and furniture, which they began to arrange and rearrange in the space. Gradually, the entire studio was transformed into the living room of the play's principal characters—a room which, during the performance, was inhabited not only by the actors but by the audience as well.

Victims of Duty was the first American "environmental" theatre production. The basic ideas behind its spatial organization which were stated after the production by Schechner in an essay called "Six Axioms for an Environmental Theatre," in *The Drama Review,* were related to concepts being developed about the same time by Jerzy Grotowski, Julian Beck and Judith Malina, Ludovico Ronconi, Peter Brook, and others. In a sense, the design principles that informed *Victims* were part of a strikingly contemporary movement, with few obvious roots in the history of Western theatre. But the movement was not without important precedents, and the environmental tradition, in fact,

Victims of Duty The main environment. Photo: Matt Herron, Black Star.

represents a far more ancient and far more common solution to the problems of organizing performance space than the critics and historians have supposed.

The environmental approach to space almost certainly first developed out of the need to adapt sites, not originally conceived of as theatres, for various kinds of performances—rituals, festivals, processions, and plays. Throughout history both indoor and outdoor spaces have been used, some left in their natural state (what the Happenings movement of the late 1950's would come to call "found environments"), and others transformed in some special way for the event which they housed. Associated with all of the variations is the idea that a single performance space may contain both actors and spectators. This kind of "environmental" performance space stands in clear contrast to that of formal theatre structures—especially those built in Europe from the Renaissance onwards—in which the actor is removed, architecturally and scenically, from his audience. In the environmental tradition, this separation has never been seen as necessary, and performance space has been viewed as a single, all-encompassing unit. The result has been that the boundaries between actor and spectator have been informal or indefinitely drawn, and there has been not only close contact but often an intermingling of the two groups.

In much traditional folk and popular performances, for example, an outdoor space not originally designed as a setting for theatre is often used for production. The space may be altered to contain platforms or stages, stations, or booths of some sort at which action takes place—sequentially or simultaneously. But the audience is relatively mobile and the action of the performance takes place not so much on stages, at stations or in booths, as in the whole environment. It is the environment itself which is the place of performance, not any of its components.

The most basic found environments used by traditional performers are those public places where a crowd is certain to gather—the streets, the beach, or the market place. In such spaces, the mummer, the seaside Pierrot, the mountebank, and the busker create informal stations—performance spaces which the showman roughly defines with a banner or a table, or merely with his costume, a musical instrument, or a few properties. These stations each become a simple matrix or center of focus for a group of spectators. There is no rigid separation beween spectators and the performer as there is in orthodox theatres, and their relationship is fluid and informal. The audience is free to watch the performance or ignore it as they please, to retreat when the hat is passed for contributions, or to drift away to a more interesting performance somewhere else in the street or market place.

The street performer does not alter the environment in which he works to any great degree. But for more complex traditional performances, like parades and processions, the streets are consciously transformed into highly theatricalized environments by a festival overlay on the ordinary functional architecture of the town. The transformation is accomplished with flags, banners, special sound and music, the costumes of the marchers, and the floats which form the nucleus of the procession. The entire procession is, in effect, a series of platforms or stages in motion within the larger environment of the town, much of which is used as an improvised auditorium.

Spectators are sometimes forced to watch the procession from behind barriers. But as in other forms of environmental performances, the audience is basically a dynamic unit—able to shift position and respond to the event with far more freedom than spectators in orthodox theatre. Sometimes direct physical involvement is encouraged and spectators become, in effect, performers. At traditional New Orleans Mardi Gras processions, for example, cheap medals and strings of beads are thrown into the crowd by costumed riders on the floats. The response is immediate and frantic; spectators surge into the procession, breaking ranks to snatch souvenirs from the air, and are only forced back onto the sidewalks by parade marchers and the policemen who line the route.

Despite his often close physical contact with the procession, much of it is missed by the typical spectator. Parts of it can scarcely be seen, and much of the accompanying sound can only be heard indistinctly, if at all. But sight and sound do not assume the same kind of significance for spectators at processional performances that they do in conventional theatres. Because of the large scale of the procession and the simplicity of the presented images, there is little need for the spectator to observe it closely; all that is really necessary is a grasp of the main thematic lines. Like other environmental performances, the procession is based less on comprehension of all the details of a single highly focused theatrical event than on the involvement of the spectator in a complex of theatrical experiences in a distinctive performance environment.

Ultimately, a parade transforms a found environment in a limited way since the original function of the space continues to coexist with the performance. At the traditional fairground, however, a found space is transformed more radically by being filled with elaborate and highly specialized performance architecture. Often this architecture is intrinsically banal. But that fact is unimportant; it is the total effect that is significant—a landscape of blazing light and brilliant color which creates a powerful, self-contained festival environment.

At European fairs and American carnivals, the streets of a town or an open field are transformed into an independent entertainment environment which masks the original function of the space. It is basically the idea of a market place: the fairground becomes a "town" in its own right with its own special character, meticulously divided into a network of subenvironments. "Open" subenvironments (rides and game stalls) may be participated in directly from the grounds, while "closed" subenvironments (the waxworks, the hall of mirrors, the fun house, and so on) must be entered by the spectator. At a typical fair, dozens of different kinds of performance events are taking place simultaneously, and the spectator creates his own unique organization of the space by his choice of certain booths, rides and stalls in a certain order as he finds his way through the larger environment of the fairground.

Boys games, Bali.

American Carnival poster. Courtesy of
Circus World Museum, Baraboo, Wisconsin.

All of the environmental spaces mentioned thus far have been connected with traditional folk and popular performance forms, many of them dating back thousands of years in time. At least a few of these traditional forms have continued to exist in Europe and America today. Some, like busking, have survived virtually intact, while others, like the Disney Parks and their imitators, are the result of the application of modern technology to the idea of the entertainment environment. Since the end of the 19th century, however, quite new environmental forms have also been developing, many of them associated with radical or avant-garde performance. In some cases, their use of space has clearly been influenced by folk and popular environments—a conscious attempt has been made to adapt traditional spatial concepts to the requirements of contemporary performance. In other cases, there has apparently been little conscious awareness of an environmental tradition, but designers have arrived at spatial solutions not very different from those used in ancient folk and popular performance.

From the agit-prop performances of the 1920's and 30's, through the informal sidewalk political sketches and guerrilla theatre of the 60's, for example, outdoor found environments—often the city streets or political demonstration sites—have been used for production. Many street groups have had relatively little interest in transforming the environment in which their performance takes place. Like traditional street performers they have frequently chosen the streets for practical rather than artistic reasons—for the most part because the space is free and there is a ready-made audience to be found.

Much of the American guerrilla theatre and political street performance of the 1960's virtually ignored orthodox design elements. In a calculated reversal of the usual artistic values, many emphasized poverty and a primitive approach to space, color, and design. A performance by a political theatre group called The Burning City Company, for example, was presented in a square outside Saint Mark's in the Bowery—a New York City East Village church closely identified with the street life and street people of the 60's. The square and the church were ignored by actors and audience alike. Spectators wandered up to the performance, forming a rough circle around the actors who were performing on, around, and under an ordinary bed sheet, tie-dyed red, and much the worse for wear. The sheet, which more or less defined the performance space, was the only scenic element—except for a few crudely painted masks attached to broom handles. The total effect was calculatedly primitive and shabby. By implication, at least, it represented an aggressive attack on orthodox theatre architecture and design through a return to the minimal stagecraft of the mountebank and the busker.

Another contemporary American group, Peter Schumann's Bread and Puppet Theatre, offers an example of a more complex handling of outdoor found space. In one sense, Schumann seemingly cares very little where Bread and Puppet productions take place. Like many other groups that are oriented toward the streets, the Bread and Puppet Theatre has usually gone where people congregate, performing in virtually any found space that can accommodate a production—on the pavements, in forests, on lawns, on the boardwalk at New York's Coney Island amusement park, and in recent years in a variety of indoor spaces. But there is an important difference between the attitude of the Bread and Puppet Theatre toward space and that of many guerrilla and street theatre groups. Schumann does not ignore the environments which he chooses for his performances; instead he negotiates with them, temporarily transforming each of them with extraordinary combinations of

movement, color, and shape. Although he works with many of the same simple and often shabby materials used by typical street groups, Schumann meticulously redesigns them. Using puppet figures, some of them almost 20 feet tall, he drastically changes the scale of the space in which he works, isolating and dominating portions of the larger environment through a mixture of procession and stational performance.

What may well have been the Bread and Puppet Theatre's most complex scenographic work took place during the summer of 1974, on a huge outdoor site—a landscape transformed as a performance environment. Called the *Domestic Resurrection Fair and Circus*, the performance was presented in the hills of Vermont in an enormous meadow. Here, Schumann staged more than 50 different performances and exhibits, using a mixture of puppets and live performers to create such events as a symbolic battle between red and white armies that spectators watched from places on the surrounding hills.

Schumann's interest in the use of broad expanses of landscape as performance environments is not an isolated one. Panoramic outdoor productions have been presented recently by Robert Wilson and Peter Brook, as well as by practitioners in the United States of "the new dance." A number of dance pieces, for example, have used the streets as environments, not from an interest in attracting passersby as spectators, but because of the choreographer's belief that a particular site or group of sites can serve as a dynamic dance background. This interest is probably influenced by the concern with found environments which grew up as part of the Happenings movement of the late 50's and early 60's, as well as by "earthworks" and other recent environmental art. The result, for example, has been dance pieces using the roofs of buildings as vantage points for spectators, spreading the action through the streets below or

Nikolai Okhlopkov's production of
Gorki's *Mother*.

over adjacent rooftops.

One recent piece choreographed by Trisha Brown, took spectators onto the roof of a loft building in a lower Manhattan warehouse district where they watched dancers dressed in red perform on the roofs of other buildings scattered over the district. The dancers transmitted a series of movements to one another, "sending" and "receiving" gestures, motions, and postures from one rooftop to another. The dancers were placed 360 degrees around the spectators' vantage point, and at varying distances from it so that it was necessary for audience members to move freely around their roof in order to discover new dancers and better positions from which to watch. Thus they became, in affect, the moving hub of a dance piece which spread out around them in all directions within the larger environment of the city.

Vessel, a dance piece by Meredith Monk, extended even farther the idea of the city as environment, using three separate and different locations for the three parts of the piece—Monk's own house, The Performance Group's Performing Garage, and a parking lot—with spectators transported by bus through the darkened streets of New York from one site to another. In *Vessel,* Monk used not only two outdoor found environments (the streets of Manhattan and the parking lot), but also an indoor found environment (Monk's living loft), and an indoor transformed environment (The Performing Garage), where the existing performance space was completely altered by draped lengths of white material.

Many 20th-century directors and designers have chosen to work with indoor environmental spaces, often using found environments because of values unique to the space or for basically pragmatic reasons. Thus in 1923-1924, Eisenstein used a genuine gas factory for a play set in a gasworks. And, in recent years, Julian Beck and Judith Malina of The Living Theatre used a huge New York auditorium, the Opera House of The Brooklyn Academy of Music, not as a conventional theatre but as a convenient environment for their *Paradise Now,* with actors and spectators mingling.

Other modern environmentalists have concentrated on transforming existing indoor spaces or on constructing totally new environments. In some cases their work has been, in effect, an extension of the 19th-century naturalist tradition, which served as a stimulus for the creation of experimental environments designed to promote a richer, more complex naturalism. In the 1930's, for example, Nikolai Okhlopkov, Artistic Director of the Realistic Theatre in Moscow, explored the possibilities of naturalism by developing a distinctive montage principle in the theatre. In his productions, Okhlopkov characteristically combined a number of separate acting areas with several audience seating areas in a single performance space. For his famous production of *Mother,* for example, Okhlopkov created not only a central arena containing a platform stage, but a peripheral stage around all four sides of the room, joined to the arena platform by runways and step units. The audience, seated in four separate sections between the central arena and the peripheral stages, was surrounded by a montage of scenes handled in a basically cinematic way, using such devices as cuts and stop action.

A more technical exploration of the possibilities of naturalism lay behind the Infinidome, a structure designed in the 1930's by an American, Blanding Sloane, but never built. The building, a huge dome, was to contain a battery of projectors like those in a planetarium, between the audience and the stage, which were to project color effects and motion pictures keyed to a

Infinidome, Blanding Sloane, 1937.

peformance on the dome. The audience thus would be surrounded with color and movement, and an elaborate system of speakers around the circumference of the dome would engulf them in sound. The Infinidome represented an early application of technology to the idea of environmental space, an application that has continued to interest architects and designers, perhaps reaching its high point in the complex multi-media pavilions of Montreal's Expo 67.

Although naturalism has informed some environmental work, anti-naturalism has been a far more potent force. Standing behind much of the 20th-century environmental design has been a desire to create alternatives to the naturalist view of the function of scene design and to the 19th-century architectural tradition which rigidly separates spectators and performers in two adjacent chambers. In the naturalist-proscenium convention, the stage house contains a distinctive reality, inhabited solely by the performers, which may be observed only at a distance through the proscenium arch by those not part of the action of the play. From time to time performers may violate the convention by leaving the stage for some reason and joining the audience. But it is conscious violation—for all intents and purposes the two territories are clearly defined architecturally, and decorated in ways that make their separate functions clear. In a sense the whole of the 20th century in Europe and America demonstrates a gradual retreat from these conventions, a retreat made clear by the development of the arena and thrust stages and the growth of various schools of design which modify or abstract the naturalist vision of reality. But a number of more radical reactions against the naturalist-proscenium idea have concentrated on replacing the two chambers with a single shared space, the whole of which is transformed scenically for the production.

The seeds of this approach were first seen in Europe in the work and theory of Appia and Meyerhold. By the 20's experiments with indoor environmental spaces were being conducted by Jacques Copeau and Michel Saint-Denis, and in 1938 Antonin Artaud's *Theatre of Cruelty* set down his vision of a new kind of environmental theatre structure. The theatre, with an audience in the center, was to be ringed with a gallery and raised platforms at the four corners of the room, thus encircling the spectators with action—a scenographic idea not unlike those of Okhlopkov, although arrived at from an anti-naturalist position about the fuction of performance space. By the 60's more radical transformations of interior space were being developed by Jerzy Grotowski of The Polish Laboratory Theatre and other

Grotowski's production of Slowacki's *Kordian*. Spectators and performers share the same space.
Photo: Edward Weglowski

European directors. The "scenic architecture" developed by Grotowski's designers from simple objects and materials has cast performers and audience in a wide variety of physical relationships, often intense and intimate ones. In his production of Slowacki's *Kordian*, for example, the playing space suggests the interior of a mental hospital, housing not only the characters in the play but spectators as well, incorporated into the action as patients at the asylum. In Grotowski's version of Wyspianski's *Akropolis* the spectators, representing the dead of Auschwitz, are seated in small groups in an environment over which is suspended a wire gridiron on which lengths of stovepipe are hung by the performers who represent live prisoners going about their tasks in the concentration camp.

In the United States an important influence on the design of recent environmental performance was the Happenings movement of the late 1950's and early 60's. The roots of the movement, which was centered in New York City, may be traced back to Dada, Surrealism, the Bauhaus, and more recently the compositions of John Cage. There was a strong influence from action painting, collage, and environment—the concept of an art work that completely surrounds the viewer, an idea already present in the art world early in the century.

By no means were all Happenings environmental in their approach to the handling of space. But because so many of those who produced Happenings came from the world of art rather than that of theatre, there was no particular commitment to orthodox theatre architecture and design—not even the commitment to radicalize it in some way. Instead, performance space was frequently conceived anew from the point of view of the painter and sculptor rather than that of the theatre director and scene designer. The result was unusual uses of space—some environmental—as well as the employment of materials more common to the artist's studio of the period than to the theatre. Thus Allan Kaprow's 1959 presentation, *18 Happenings in 6 Parts* took place in the Reuben Gallery, a former loft in New York's East Village, which was transformed for the Happening into three separate chambers with walls made of raw wooden frameworks covered with translucent plastic sheeting. Open doorways in each of the chambers provided access to a corridor created along one side of the gallery. The walls of the chambers, which did not extend to the gallery ceiling, were topped in two of the rooms with strings of light bulbs, alternately red and white, mounted about a foot apart. A third room was illuminated by a blue bulb hanging from the ceiling and an arrangement of colored lights on one wall. At various points were collages using such material as torn canvas, pieces of theatrical gelatin, and artificial fruit, and in two of the rooms full-length mirrors reflected reversed images of the spaces and the activities taking place in them. Seating for spectators was arranged differently in each of the chambers and the audience progressed from one chamber to another during the course of the Happening, although the events taking place in other rooms where always vaguely visible.

Many of the scenographic qualities of presentations like *18 Happenings in 6 Parts* carried over into the design of later American environmental theatre pieces, joining with ideas from the European environmental tradition to produce unique transformations of indoor performance spaces. The productions designed by Jerry Rojo for plays directed by Richard Schechner at The Performing Garage in New York City have been set in some of the most complex and extensive of these environments.

The room in which the performances take place is a simple unornamented space about 50 feet long, 35 feet wide and 20

Grotwoski's production of *Akropolis.*
The final scene.

feet high. For each of the productions at the Garage the room is transformed in some way—largely through the use of wooden and metal construction—to create an environment which stems out of the work of the performers in the play presented and houses both performers and spectators, who often are free to move at will throughout the space. Typical of all of Rojo's transformations is a conscious attempt at asymmetry—the creation of irregular platforms, gangways, cubby-holes, tunnels, "secret" spaces, and the like—and an interest in working with basic structures of raw wood, rope, and unpolished metal, allowing the materials to make their own statements as wood, metal, or rope rather than attempting to mask their functions by converting them into conventional pieces of stage scenery.

Structures built for one production may be redesigned later for another, but the use of the space and the complex of shapes placed within it differs widely from one Performance Group production to another. Thus the environment for Schechner's production of *Dionysus in 69*, an adaptation of Euripides' *The Bacchae*, consisted mainly of a number of stark, rather open wooden towers grouped in a rough circle around an open floor area covered in black rubber mats, while his next environment, for an adaptation of Shakespeare's *Macbeth*, employed a very confined entrance tunnel, and a complicated arrangement of small and constricted "cabins" rising around a central "table." In another production, much of the floor space of the Garage was occupied by a giant "wave" made of plywood, and more recently the center of the floor contained a complex of towers and bridges jointly occupied by actors and audience.

It may be argued, as some critics have, that approaches to space like these destroy the unity of a performance. Indeed, it is apparent that they ignore most modern European and American ideas about seeing and hearing and most orthodox concepts about such subjects as audience seating, the relationship of actor and spectator, and the function and appearance of scenic design. But it may also be argued that the approach is by no means a bizarre or eccentric one—merely that it is different from that seen in the mainstream of modern theatre architecture, continuing in its own way an older tradition about the organization of performance space—the environmental tradition.

Jerry Rojo Some Principles and Concepts of Environmental Design

The majority of concepts developed by a theatre artist over the course of a career should have little practical meaning for anyone other than himself. Let me begin by stating that I resist the idea of presenting a set of abstract rules or axioms that presume to outline universal ways of theatre. It has been said that any theatre artist is a criminal who ultimately adheres to no established laws or methods; indeed he destroys, then creates anew in each venture. The strongest work evolves from an individual artist who possesses a private unique vision about what he does. He spends a lifetime in pursuit of that vision (someone said it takes ten years of work before anybody knows what he is doing) and each work consists of *ways of doing* or *concepts*. For the artist, concepts exist on three levels: a way of doing life, a way of doing theatre, film, TV, etc., and a way of doing a specific work or project. There is a certain unity of transactions among these three levels, but in a relative way it is possible only to examine the concepts around a specific work. It seems to me that only if each work is dealt with on its own terms can we come to know about it in a meaningful way. For me each theatre assignment consists of a continuum of problems to be solved in view of some vision. Rather than attempting to catalogue "truths" about environmental theatre I prefer to talk about specific projects, the theory and concepts out of which they grew.

Perhaps it would be worthwhile to define environmental theatre as I understand it and as it is reflected in my own work. Environmental theatre in the broadest sense has come to mean for me an organic production process in which an ensemble of performers, writers, designers, directors, and technicians participate on a regular basis in the formation of the piece through workshops and rehearsals. The ensemble may itself compose the text or *mise en scene* as in the Performance Group's *Commune*; an ensemble may perform the work of a writer not connected to the group as in Shaliko's production of Ibsen's *Ghosts*; or a writer may be in residence with the ensemble as in Jean-Claude van Itallie's collaboration with The Open Theatre's *The Serpent*. In the idea of the *mise en scene*, or living action in time and space, the environmentalist begins with the notion that the production will both develop from, and totally inhabit, a given space; and that, for the performer and audience, time, space, and materials exist as what they are and only for their intrinsic value. All aesthetic problems are solved in terms of actual time, space, and materials with little consideration given to solutions that suggest illusion, pretense, or imitation.

In the more traditional theatre experience, the production is appreciated from outside, in a world especially created for the relatively passive observer. In the environmental experience, on the other hand, appreciation generates from within by virtue of shared activity. Each environmental production creates a sense of total involvement on the part of the audience and performer. There is a sense of the immediate in which the principle "suspension of disbelief" does not apply. With the notion "suspension of disbelief" the audience is asked to believe that an artificial event is actually happening as it is *acted*; whereas in environmental theatre the audience believes the event is actually happening because it is *performed* and there is no question of make-believe. Also important to the environmentalist is the notion that environmental theatre places heavy emphasis on physicalization rather than verbalization. In addition to the shared activity between audience and performer in traversing complex space, there is a new awareness of the performers' potential in physicalization. The environmental theatre space encourages dramatic action and

Sam Shepard's *The Tooth of Crime*, The Performance Group production. Hoss talks to Cheyenne. Photo: Clem Fiori

activity that is in the form of "signs" and body language.

Some words about kinds of space. The title of this book is *Theatres, Spaces, Environments*. In effect, for the purpose of this book, the three terms are synonymous. The orthodox physical theatre arrangement has the audience in fixed relationship to a stage area because the stagehouse is used to create illusion and spectacle, and the distancing is necessary for these effects. Also, the bifurcated space of auditorium, stage, lobby are each designed for autonomous functions. In the environmental theatre there is a tendency to unify these areas or at least arrange them so that the spaces seem to transform one into the other. The facilities in an environmental theatre are utilitarian in purpose, in that they help change space relationships and serve to augment performer activity. Therefore, with each production the entire complex is transformed in appearance or feeling to suit the needs of the particular piece. Thus the theatre, space, and environment are one and the same and change for each production.

Many of these theatres developed from existing spaces such as churches, gymnasiums, and halls and are referred to as "open space" theatres. They are without fixed seating, accommodating no more than a few hundred people and are fitted out with rudimentary lighting and rigging. The Performing Garage is an example of such a converted space. Formerly a metal stamping factory in an industrial district of New York City, The Performing Garage consists of a room with no fixed seats, 50' long, 35' wide, and 19' high. A new environment is constructed in the room for each new production. The room contains a simple and flexible lighting system, consisting of a metal gridiron which covers the entire ceiling and from which lighting instruments are suspended; outlets for plugging instruments are located throughout the room; and there is a very simple lighting control board with six dimmers, and a total capacity of 15,000 watts.

It is becoming increasingly common for regional, university, and commercial theatre complexes to include—along with more conventional proscenium and thrust stage theatres—an "open space" theatre on the order of The Performing Garage for environmental or other experimental productions. The most recent theatres (sometimes called "black box theatres") are no longer improvised rooms developed out of existing spaces, but completely new structures designed with environmental principles in mind.

Variations from the usual "open space" environmental design are represented by new theatres at Sarah Lawrence College near New York City and at the University of Connecticut. The theatres are built according to a concept which I have called "fixed environments theatre." In this concept the attempt is to provide a *permanent* environment used for all productions, consisting of varied levels, companionways, and stairs, used both by audience and actors. Here, as in the "open space" concept, where the environment changes with each production, there is no fixed seating. Rather, different parts of the "fixed or permanent environment" are used for both audience seating areas and acting areas during each new production. Spectators may sit on edge of platforms, or on movable benches, or they may "float" freely from one part of the theatre to another depending on the dictates of the production.

While the fixed environmental theatre seems to contradict the principle of a new organic space for each production, in practice there is no inconsistency. I have directed a number of pieces in the UConn Mobius Theatre and have found that while the disposition of areas is physically fixed there is a psychic

difference for each space within the environment depending on how it is used. The inherent neutrality of the overall space is open for reinterpretation with each production. Also, we have in some more conventional productions effectively added scenic elements to the environment—changing the appearance.

The scope of the environmental designer's responsibility extends to organizing the total space, selecting materials, determining construction techniques, and considering the associational and intrinsic value of each aspect of design. The traditional bifurcated space of lobby, stage, technical areas, backstage, and auditorium are, in this kind of theatre, no longer considered to be immutable, but are subject to organization and reorganization according to a particular production concept. Traditionally, spatial arrangements are imposed on a production, as in theatres with fixed seating. The environmentalist, however, feels that aesthetic considerations should determine movement and actor-audience arrangements.

Typically the environmental designer's impulse begins with architectural and engineering considerations because he has to serve a new kind of physically oriented actor-director, an actively participating audience, and a concept that views space, time and action in terms of an immediate living experience. Therefore, the designer is concerned with the total disposition of space and its related problems—not only problems of production, but also those involved with building codes, safety, comfort, public services, and the peculiar engineering and construction difficulties that arise when a whole complex of theatre experiences is placed under one roof. Thus, in the environmental production, the interaction and negotiation between performers and audience requires a sharing of facilities which implies not so much stage design but architecture. In essence, the designer becomes a hybrid architect-designer who conceives of a totally new theatre for each production.

One fundamental concept that shapes the environmental theatre production is that it is usually approached using the principle of unity of time, place, and action. And the immediacy of this concept suggests that environmental theatre productions are experienced organically from *within* the total space. In the space, the performers and audience members perceive and interact with the piece in individual ways. Traditionally, the audience experiences the production safely at a distance, as if it were part of a puzzle which must be put into the correct place if the director's intentions are to be correctly realized. In environmental theatre, however, each audience member, in his own way, works with and is integrated into the production. The same is true for the actors, whose function in the space is more active than that of the spectator but essentially similar.

The function of lighting in environmental theatre illustrates how a production is experienced from within. When the audience is separated from the production, as in the proscenium theatre or the cinema, the lighting is designed to provide a more or less two-dimensional, picture-frame unifying effect. The concept is based on the idea of composing pictures that move with time. In such cases, the lighting exists as a kind of layered effect; that is, on top of the performer and in between the audience and performer. Traditionally, light is used to affect the brain through eye sensation. Environmental theatre lighting, however, engages other senses as well. One can approach light, retreat from it, feel light, even smell it. Environmental theatre lighting is not used to create unity,

balance, rhythm, and the like, through pictorial organization; it is used as *activity* within a constantly changing and fugitive space in a living theatre situation.

An example is the use of light in The Manhattan Project's production of *Endgame*. The environment consisted of a hexagonal-shaped performing area that is about 26' in diameter; the audience was seated around the six-sided arena, on two levels; these levels were divided into stall-like cubicles that accommodated two to four people; a companionway behind the stalls allowed the audience access into their cubicles. Separating the audience members from performers was a 12' high wire screen which, when lighted properly, prevented the performer from seeing the audience but allowed the audience to clearly see the actors. The screen also prevented the audience from seeing the mass of audience members on the opposite side of the playing area. The "wall" of light and the stall-like cubicles for the audience served in an active way to allow each spectator to "tune in" or "tune out" at will, and privately, the content of the production. Further, the use of light provided insulation for the audience who viewed the production as if they were witness to the activities of a scabrous and repugnant group of inmates from some madhouse. On the other hand, the performer could interact with the "wall-of-light cage" effect of the environment because it served to augment the feeling of human isolation important to their performance. The four characters of the play are the last of humanity engaged in an end-game just before the void sets in. For them the lighted screen/cage became a real barrier to the cosmic void beyond. Throughout this production the lighting was generated in a concrete way from *within* and interacted with the audience and performer.

In Shaliko's production of *Ghosts* at the Public Theatre in New

The Manhattan Project's production of
Samuel Beckett's *Endgame*. The
audience is separated from the performers by a 12' high wire screen.
Photo: Babette Mangolte

York, the lighting, props and spatial arrangement all worked to generate internal activity for audience/performer. To encourage an historical environmental reality for audience/performer there was an authentic use of props and light. The lighting was created by using period practical electric light fixtures (1910) to achieve a natural incandescent light. And the performers were directed to actually control the illumination for the play. The audience was set in clusters around the room on various levels to suggest the rooms and walls of an Edwardian mansion.

It is interesting to note that environmental designs are not readily translated into pictorial renderings that depict mood or idea. This is because these productions exist in concepts which rely on transactions among audience, performer, text, time and space; and are therefore, only perceived internally during production.

Another concept at work in environmental theatre is the use of production elements that originate from non-matrixed or abstract exploration. Most theatrical use of props, space, costume, and light derives from historical or common usage sources. That is, there is a matrix or common information of how something is used. A chair historically is designed to be occupied in a certain logical manner. The non-matrixed use of a chair may find it turned into, say, a costume and thus may be worn instead of sat in. This non-matrixed or alogical use of a prop does not try to imitate the use of a prop as seen in society, but represents an attempt to use props as agents for discovery through accident, chance and intuition. Using a non-matrixed approach to production provides an open-ended use of elements around us.

An example of a non-matrixed use of a costume-prop is seen in

The Big Enchilada, an adaptation of *Ubu Roi*, staged in the Mobius Theatre at the University of Connecticut. One of the performers playing an Ubu-like military tyrant used a Kodak Instamatic flash camera as a "weapon," and part of his costume was made up of a Mexican-bandit-crossed-bullet-belt. Instead of bullets he carried an arsenal of flash cubes. The camera-flashing motif used throughout the production helped to establish the performer's character relationship to Watergate activities, Madison Avenue public relations, and the military complex, in one fell swoop.

Shaliko's version of Ibsen's *Ghosts* using only practical lighting. Photo: Nathaniel Tileston

Mother Courage played by Joan MacIntosh in The Performance Group production wearing a costume which includes a parachute harness. Photo: Clem Fiori

In the same production a performer playing a ghostlike seductress performed a ballet nude with flashlights strapped to her wrists. Delivering fragments of Shakespearean ghost dialogue she danced among the audience with only the light from the flashlights reflecting off her body and the space around her. As in this production, lighting effects used in performance are generally discovered in process of workshops and rehearsal rather than being logically preconceived at the outset. In effect, such "unnatural" non-matrixed use of light is an act of confrontation or transgression because the unnatural effect initiates a trauma that ultimately draws attention to itself. Here one thinks of Brecht's concept of alienation and Grotowski's idea of transgression.

The environmentalist is preoccupied with extracting and exploiting the intrinsic qualities of materials and space. From this sensitivity to the nuances of the characteristics of materials there develops an entire logic based on the associative and connotative value of things around us. For example, a performer may choose to use the warming quality of light—the simple fact that the temperature is higher inside the light than outside—or he may select the crisp edge of a sharp-focused ellipsoidal spotlight to delineate territory. In such a pragmatic approach there is an attempt to exploit the salient features of the lighting equipment and the possibilities offered by light itself. In environmental theatre there is an emphatic move away from using materials to create illusion, promote deception, or theatrical surprises, to instead accepting material in an unaltered or undisguised manner. This practical approach to materials suggests that materials have their own psychic energy and which exists by itself and not only for the production as is the tradition. In this case, actors are trained to negotiate with and develop private associations with materials.

Using lighting as an example, it is not unique to environmental theatre to employ the intrinsic and associative value of light since historical plays such as *Othello*, *The Three Sisters*, and the work of such practitioners as Brecht, Meyerhold, Craig, and Appia all suggest strong use of the associative value of light. When, in the second act of *The Three Sisters*, Natasha carries a candle light alone she is foreshadowing her takeover of the household. The playwright clearly intends that light and power are to be associated. It must be noted, however, that historically this use of light often was relegated, like sub-text, to a position of relative minor importance in order to maintain the rigors of realism or to make the play conform to some other stylistic mode. By comparison, in the environmental theatre *mise en scene* the use of associative values of materials is presented openly and conspicuously. In the production of *Baal Games,*an adaptation of Brecht's *Baal* performed by the Mobius Ensemble at the University of Connecticut,the actor playing Ekart was associating with images of sun, clouds, air and light. Consequently this light-complected, blond-haired actor in white clothing did much of his performing in proximity to light and high places. For example, he may be seen casting shadows on the other performers or bathing in light as if to take on energy from it. The Performance Group's production of *Mother Courage* utilized an extensive system of ropes and block and tackle as a metaphor for the use of the wagon. Instead of using a literal wagon of merchandise, Mother Courage and her children were often fettered to the myriad of ropes and pulleys and were free to associate with being tied down or manipulated. In environmental theatre, the actor necessarily uses elements of *mise en scene* for motivational and associative purposes in ways and means not found in other forms of theatre.

Traditionally young designers are taught to be jacks of all trades. They are taught to be capable of a range of design styles and problems—musicals, box sets, scene painting, decor, portrait painting, electronics, props, etc. As Moliere pointed out ,"one who masters all, masters none." I feel there should be a deep art and art appreciation training, and subsequent study in theatre history and styles. However, soon a selective elimination process should take place. One in which the designer begins to focus and become committed to a style of work. Taking a cue from painters and sculptors—who spend long periods of their life exploring specific problems—the stage designer needs not to see himself in servitude to every play and project that comes along, but accept only those that foster some vision and discovery.

Richard Schechner   **Environmentalists Now**

By 1965 it seemed that big permanent changes were coming to the theatre. The intersection of four avenues of change pressed theatre into a new phase. On one side were the various Movements—black, student, sexual, feminist, anti-War—creating in America a sense that the streets were authentic stages, a common legislature where common people—acting as agents of "participatory democracy" might effect with pageantry, passion, and theatre what they could not achieve through the "regular channels" of lobbying and secret pressure.

Who can forget the climactic month of May 1970 when, at Kent State, the National Guard (out of panic, or with forethought?) used live ammunition on students protesting the invasion of Cambodia, killing four of them? Since then the campuses have gotten very quiet, students (we are told) are "serious about their studies." And the new buildings designed since the 60's are veritable fortresses, with few windows on the ground floors, easily controlled ports of entry, rigidly fixed seating. Nowhere is the reactionary fear of the administrators (nationally, locally, educationally) more visible than in the new campus architecture.

Or take Richard Nixon's reaction to the 100,000 plus people who stormed into Washington that May to protest Cambodia and Kent State. He ordered dozens of old D.C. buses drawn up in a bumper-to-bumper circle around the White House. It was a scene out of Hollywood Westerns: the covered wagons drawn up in a circle around the settlers, the outraged Indians racing around hollering and getting shot (in Washington with tear-gas). So Nixon saw himself in relation to the mostly young protestors. But over the next few years he had his way with them; subverting, harrassing, jailing, murdering, and co-opting their leadership, effectively reducing protest to impotence by

isolating and driving to fanatical extremes those who offered a radical critique of American social order. Only at the end did some Middle Americans realize that Nixon was the most un-American of all; and that even before his administration the government had been taken over by corporate fascists. Nixon's error was *hubris*: he expedited illegally what the others were very effectively doing within laws as flexible as banlon. So Nixon was dumped. Shakespeare would have loved the plot.

The streets were activated from desperation: where else can we go? Protest moved "on location," just like the movies. Go where it hurts and show them how you feel: soda-fountain counters, bathrooms, the Pentagon, public schools, Mississippi, the railroad tracks across which arms are shipped, the office of the administrator. A definite actual, ritual, pageant theatre was born. A street and guerrilla theatre designed at once to express and to release the needs and passions of thousands of participant-performers. Some groups like the San Francisco Mime Troupe, the Bread and Puppet Theatre, the Pageant Players, the Free Southern Theatre, the Living Theatre—and scores of ad-hoc guerrilla theatres took up staging what hurt immediately, of bringing people to consciousness in two ways: by giving the performers something to do and by directly confronting those who had done harm. The media—especially TV—would bring the news to the rest of the population. It was an updated version of the Living Newspapers of the 30's. But with TV bringing picture-news instantly, there was no need to wait even a day, or to take texts from the *New York Times.* (People learned it was likely that the networks made the news it reported. On all sides, ordinary life—or those parts of it that people found exciting and dramatic—was staged.) Many events were planned in order to stimulate the media, especially TV. Anyone who participated in a protest knows that "getting the networks to cover it" was maybe the most important thing.

The idea of an event with a double purpose is built into the theory of guerrilla theatre. To be effective guerrilla theatre, an event has to be *both* authentic (here and now, felt, actual) and staged (packaged, made so that the media is interested in filming and broadcasting it, designed for a "broader audience"). The events must be newsworthy, meaning they need flash, compressed into a few seconds, making their statement clearly. They can't unfold like Ibsen, they have to explode like an ad for Burger King. (Some of the extended dramas and hermetic imagery in the work of Robert Wilson and Richard Foreman are, I think, reactions against this pressure to compress and simplify.) All too soon guerrilla theatre didn't need any purpose beyond getting the attention of the public; the style came to dominate the content. This is what Robert Brustein calls "News Theatre."

It is news theater when a California family agrees to expose before television cameras the most intimate secrets of its family life, including marital strife and divorce and the homosexual inclinations of one of the children. It is news theater when the Symbionese Liberation Army kidnaps the daughter of a newspaper magnate and then designs its every move to capture and dominate the media, whether through publicity for a food distribution program, or its demand to have two imprisoned members appear on television, or its choice of a bank with automatic cameras so that a robbery can be photographically recorded (the apocalyptic demise of six members of the S.L.A. in a flaming Los Angeles house, as seen on television, is also a form of news theater). It is news theater when Arab guerrillas are able to command the attention of the world's media by assassinating 11 members of the Israeli Olympic team or by blowing up a hijacked airliner or by gunning down innocent children in a Maalot schoolhouse.[2]

The progression goes: the media tire of theatre—even of "media freaking" as practiced by Abbie Hoffman and Jerry Rubin in the 60's. What the media fed on was the real thing. And the only real thing guaranteed to get their attention was actual violence. There is no way the media can ignore an assassination, a kidnapping, a bombing. And when these events are not in themselves effective they remain effective as a way of bringing to the attention of those who watch the media the claims, or at least the hurt, of those staging and those receiving the violence.

At one time late in the 60's theatre people tried to present "as art" blood rituals. Paul Nitsch staged his Orgies Mysteries Theatre where he attempted to bring on "abreactions" in spectators by immersing bodies, especially genitals, in animal blood and guts; Ralph Ortiz destroyed pianos and slaughtered chickens; a California artist had himself shot while an audience watched. But these events revolted many people. They were decadent: an attempt to locate feeling by applying ever-increasing doses of violence.

On the other hand those who appeared with an authentic political program—such as the PLO and the IRA—were given media time no matter how bloody their actions. As terrorist organizations were legitimatized, guerrilla theatre, like guerrilla warfare, became an accepted way of getting attention to force change. The media has no qualms about showing the PLO in action or the murderous police assault on the SLA in Los Angeles simply because these "exemplary actions" (designed not only to achieve immediate ends but to tell those watching the depth of committment of those performing the action) are in fact news—they participate not in the aesthetic realm but in the actual one of ordinary life. But is it so easy to separate ordinary life from theatricalized reality? In terrorist actions the performers are selected for their theatrical effect. Patricia Hearst is kidnapped because she is the heir to the Hearst Corporation; Israeli Olympic athletes are murdered because they represent the cream of Israeli youth and because the Olympics supposedly represent international cooperation and the healing of nationalistic wounds.

A division broke the guerrilla theatre movement into three— sometimes overlapping but more often fundamentally disa- greeing—segments. Political action groups use the techniques of guerrilla theatre, just as guerrilla theatre originally used the techniques of terrorist warfare.[3] Others, as sincere in their beliefs as the terrorists, but with an aversion to violence have formed into religious communities such as the Hari Krishna sect who depend on public showings of their faith to instill unity and attract new converts. And finally there are those working in more or less traditional theatre ways such as the Teatro Campesino and the San Francisco Mime Troupe. The number of these traditional groups is diminishing because on one side they are losing to those who offer a complete life experience (political or religious) while on the other side they lose members to careers in the "professional theatre." The base which theatre stands on, putting into an histrionic frame any and all human experience, is being cut away. The frame is now provided by the TV screen, or it is removed altogether by those who argue that life itself is forever in flux. The eclecticism and skepticism of theatre, its basic farce (which is skepticism and atheism in action), is absent in political action groups and religious sects. Farce remains in groups like the Campesino or the Mime Troupe.

To summarize: A tap root of environmental theatre came from the Movements; this root has now been divided against itself forcing people to choose between political, religious, and theatrical actions. At one time it appeared as if these could be fused, or that communication could be maintained among them. Such a moment, or phase, may return; but it is not here now.

A second avenue of change came in from music and painting, and from "art theatre"—dada, futurism, surrealism. Those who invented Happenings include John Cage (musician), Allan Kaprow (painter), Claes Oldenburg (painter-sculptor), Michael Kirby (sculptor, theatre director). Cage said: "I try to make definitions that won't exclude. I would simply say that theatre is something which engages both the eye and the ear ... The reason I want to make my definition of theatre that simple is so one could view everyday life itself as theatre." Note Cage said life *could* be so viewed, not that it *had* to be.[4] His definition is truly open. Erving Goffman puts the same impulse this way: "All the world is not, of course, a stage, but the crucial ways in which it isn't are not easy to specify." [5]

Happenings don't need stories, characters, or trained professional performers. They don't need regular theatre spaces. Using chance techniques, alogical and non-matrixed performing styles artists developed a theatrical style separate from both naturalism and the reactions against naturalism (Jarry, Meyerhold, Artaud, the Absurd). The playwright as a craftsman of words was replaced by the composer-director who crafted the entire space and the events within the space. Or rules and permutations were devised whereby events happened. This same idea is current in the New Dance,[6] and the theatre of Richard Foreman and Robert Wilson. More on them later.

Happenings, like political theatre, opened vastly the range of what performance was. Anything could be framed as theatre, perceived that way; and anything could be made the subject-object of theatre. Naturalism opened theatre compared to the sentimental and heroic forms that preceded it, but naturalism was still hemmed in by conventions of staging, narrative, characterization, dialogue. Happenings made possible a formal as well as thematic expansion of the theatrical range. Also like political theatre, Happenings were affected by media, especially TV. We haven't yet integrated the idea of theatre in the bedroom, living room, or dining room—a theatre whose most dominant formal element is its fragmentation. Commercials of course out-flash the programs they purportedly sponsor; they fragment these programs. In their internal style commercials employ quick-cut, voice-over, stop-action, animation, and condensation—further fragmentations and radical stylizations of ordinary experience. Yet TV is there, in the heart of the home, it is part of ordinary experience. The use of mixed means, repetition, and stereotype on TV is much different than traditional theatre. The consistency and grace which characterizes theatre (even the Theatre of the Absurd, the last significant literary movement in theatre) is abandoned by the commercials, and by the New Theatre[7] which has been so influenced, technically, by commercials. Happenings and their successor experiments have gloried in mixing metaphors, activities, media and styles. But while accepting the technical adventure of TV the New Theatre rejects the message delivered on the surface of the commercials. An irony regarding American life-styles (as practiced by Middle America) informs the New Theatre which suggests, just as the political theatre proclaims, a radical critique of the American way.

At the same time Happenings, at least as Kaprow and Oldenburg did them, contained strong rhythms of ritual and life-endorsement, even the endorsement of aspects of life people find dull or distasteful. One of Kaprow's Happenings (a typical one whose form is duplicated many times) has people move a stack of empty barrels from one location to another, re-stacking them, re-painting them, and photographing among the barrels in triumphant poses. This process is repeated over three days until the barrels are returned to where they were first picked up and painted their original color. The basic structure of this Happening is analagous to the industrial assembly line: the repetition of an activity which seems to have no purpose; the development of a certain local feeling of community and achievement, though the whole process is fundamentally repetitious. The Happening also has the feel of a ritual—a sense of celebrating common things, which is so important too in Oldenburg's work.

In a long poem written in the style of Walt Whitman, Oldenburg begins:

I am for an art that is political-erotical-mystical, that does something other than sit on its ass in a museum.

I am for an art that grows up not knowing it is art at all, an art given the chance of having a starting point of zero.

I am for an art that embroils itself with everyday crap & still comes out on top.

I am for an art that imitates the human, that is comic, if necessary, or violent, or whatever is necessary.

I am for an art that takes its form from the lines of life itself, that twists and extends and accumulates and spits and drips, and is heavy and coarse and blunt and sweet and stupid as life itself.[8]

Happenings and their successor styles made it respectable to stop and watch a building being constructed and to think of that activity as a performance; or to introduce dialogue into dance and well-crafted whole-body movements into theatre; or to seek under the meaning of actions for action's rhythms, patterns, and repetitions: to conceive of performance as a ritual activity viewed not in strictly religious terms, or in terms of Western religion (with its anthropomorphic gods), but in ethological terms—as a pattern of behavior, as a collaboration between human beings and the other beings that inhabit the planet, even beings inanimate, artificial, and imaginary.

The third avenue of change at this environmental theatre intersection is an appetite for non-Western cultures, especially those that integrate visual arts, theatre, music, and dance; and those that have preserved a connection between their art and the rest of their lives. It is another aspect of the move toward ordinariness—but this time in the opposite direction. If naturalism (which, of course, I am suggesting was the previous big change in theatre history) tended to make everything as "sordid as real life" (as those who attacked naturalism were habitually saying), then the New Theatre wanted often to make all life as important, relevant, connected, authentic, and whole (to use some favorite words of the past 10 years) as a genuine religious experience. To find models for this kind of art—an art which sacralized everyday experience, a performing art of a very wide range of experience, people looked outside of Western culture: To native American rituals, to Asian performance—especially Indian, Balinese, Indonesian, and Japanese (cut off as we were from China, and the changes reshaping that society), less so but still important influences from Africa— a definite identification of art with whole life experiences.
Africa was decisive for black theatre, both as an original source

for its style and as a new input. But black theatre, like elements of the radical left, was systematically split off from the avant garde, so that by the start of the 70's two kinds of alternative theatre existed. And then with the rise of chicano theatre—now an important force in New York, the West Coast, and the Southwest—three kinds of alternatives each went their own way. It appears possible that by the end of this decade some degree of collaboration among these theatres is probable. I can't separate my wish for such a rapprochment from my sense of its happening. On the other hand, it's clear that black and chicano theatre are environmental—they draw on folk and religious forms, on labor organizations and field-work that use space flexibly, involve the audience in participation, take place anywhere, and demand a whole-body whole-life committment.

The ritual theatre of non-Western cultures feeds our own experiments in several ways. First it shows that what we traditionally do is not the only possibility. This is crucial because sometimes, immersed in our own history, our squabbles and developments, a hopelessness of inevitability, of social destiny, crushes our plans. Then seeing a New Guinea people celebrating an initiation, or dancing when pigs grow to slaughtering size—seeing these celebrations involve them in *both* economic and aesthetic exchanges, and recognizing that the whole of the community is participating in these performances, stamping the dances with individual style, variations, and personal expressions—recognizing this renews hope in our own theatre. Obviously the way to develop our own ritual theatre is not to import or museumify actions from other parts of the world. That appetite for bringing everything to Carnegie Hall or the Brooklyn Academy of Music is a tourist approach and not at a deep enough level to do much good (though it doesn't do much harm either). What has begun is an analysis of the structures of non-Western art, how these works are tied into social life, what life-rhythms are paralleled in the art. It is possible to do the same with our own social life and invent or discover patterns that revivify our existences.

I recognize that this sounds like a very romantic program. And the skeptic in me (he is a very real person) sneers. "If the art isn't already there you can't create it. What you're talking about is inventing procedures to simulate religious experience. It can't be done." I think it can be done. I think I am one of those engaged in trying to do it. For example, in *Mother Courage* the supper served after Scene 3 in the center of the performance was on the one hand like dinner theatre and on the other a communion built into the flow of Brecht's play. It also brought performers and spectators close together on a social plane so that the second part of the performance—and it was a long performance of nearly four hours—could start from a basis of people knowing each other, knowing that the play being performed was not an illusion but a story being told, being acted by people much like themselves; that the whole space had been used not only to tell this story but to share food. I took what I had seen in Asia, and what the Bread and Puppet Theatre did symbolically at the end of each of their performances, share bread, and built it in at the deepest structural level of *Mother Courage*. However, it wasn't sentimental: we charged $1.99 for the supper, we made it part of the story even as it broke away from the chronicle of Courage's struggle to survive.[9]

The fourth avenue of change for the theatre is the media. In moving so decisively to the center of the entertainment industry, it has helped redefine theatre as a person-to-person art, an art where change and process is at the center of the experience, where a relatively small performer-to-spectator ratio is desirable (I prefer a maximum of one performer to every 20 spectators). The media imitates contact and ironically trains people to be non-responsive. To watch monks burning to death, or real wars, or the assaults of police on the hideouts of radicals, or to experience the countless interviews with friends of those murdered, or mugging victims—to experience the distress of people not in a tragic frame, or a farcical frame, both of which relate the experience to larger ethical schemes—is training in passivity. Film and video give an illusion of actuality because the material projected is selected from actuality. And most people own cameras (still or movie) so the equipment is not esoteric. The stuff on TV is continuous with home movies and everyday events — and it is all action (action, something new, the rush of things that the media are after). Seeing so much high-powered stuff and not being able to do anything, even react directly to the suffering person so that the sufferer at least sees human concern not the passive lens of a camera, the thrust tube of a microphone—dulls the spectator's responses, flattens out the world. "The success of drama in anesthetizing our social impulses is apparent on any city street corner," says Philip Slater.[10] But his is too simple an analysis. Media actually combines with the deterioration of urban life to induce the narcosis Slater talks about. What the avant garde has been doing these past 15 years is to react against that by developing performances that train people—both performers and spectators—to do things: to move; to react; to examine the work in order to get the most out of it, to make a physical effort of doing and to enjoy this effort (just as sports are enjoyed). The performer is asked not only to "play a role" but to invent the role, to examine the role she is assigned, to reject the assignment in a creative way by developing alternatives.

The work is hard because people are very drugged. They don't want to be awakened. They sleep the sleep of prisoners.

But a dialectical process is at work. As people drop out of actual experience—as the media trains a population in passivity—people sometimes react by intervening in aesthetic events. If everyday life begins to look like theatre, theatre looks like everyday life; and if action is useless in world events, if you can't put your hand through the tube and shake the person speaking at the other end, you can stop a performance, move to take a different view of it (be your own camera). Theatre and life approach each other in terms of their effect on the audience and a definite trend is visible from the past 15 years. A convergence on the middle is happening.

Traditional Western Theatre → Media / News Theatre / News / Street Theatre / Environmental Theatre / New Dance / Happenings / Audience Participation ← Ordinary Reality

A collapse toward the middle has happened. The "in here/out there" separation which entered Western theatre at the close of the medieval period reaching its apex in the fixed proscenium theatre, and the feeling of "we're in this together" of ordinary (unmediated) reality have both disintegrated leaving a sense of separation from ordinary events ("It's just like being at a movie") *and* in conclusion, even intervention in live theatre events ("Let me do something too").

At least this is the way it works out in theory. A good deal of support can be found in contemporary performances too. Robert Wilson's long pieces—especially *Ka Mountain* (seven days) and *The Life and Times of Joseph Stalin* (12 hours) involve audiences in a way totally new for modern Western theatre. The committment is to the pattern or overall rhythm of the performance. Wilson allows for selective attention. The commandment "pay attention" which is architecturally built into the rigid up-facing seating, the uni-directional front-looking, the focus downward into the picture frame is transcended by Wilson's work. When he performs outside (*Ka Mountain*) the picture frame is gone, the landscape of Iran and the task of climbing the mountain, finding figures and events on the way up, becomes the performance. People drop in, drop out. The performance itself—which is in fact a pilgrimage—an attempt to involve the entire body in an action which replaces focused attention with an overall body-demand—in *Ka Mountain* it's not important that a spectator see everything but that she do the mountain climbing in order to see whatever it is she chooses to see. At the Brooklyn Academy of Music, the problem and solution were different. Working in the Opera House, an orthodox 2200 seat proscenium theatre replete with side boxes and two balconies, there was no question of eliminating the architectural injunction to look straight ahead and pay attention. Instead this intention was subtly and totally subverted by staging a performance that was not only too long to be stared down but that unfolded at such a slow pace as to stimulate a variety of associations within the spectators (this one at least). So that, like the musical festivals in Madras which I attended in 1972, and like much traditional theatre in Asia and Africa, the spectator finds her own way through the material, moving in and out of the space, looking for favorite passages. In the Leperque space adjoining the Opera House a canteen was set up and always throughout the night people were there talking, meeting friends, commenting on the performance. No intermission had occurred: spectators were creating their own intermissions, and thereby structuring *Stalin* themselves, actually building the experience out of the material Wilson's troupe offered. This is an example of environmental theatre conceptions being translated from the sphere of space into the sphere of time.

Other extensions and variations are being tried. In 1972 Peter Brook took his group through parts of Africa. They didn't perform set works, or tour in the usual sense. Instead they arrived in villages, introduced themselves, and discussed the possibilities of performing and exchanging performances with the villagers. It is perhaps not easy for people accustomed to American ways to understand the nature of this exchange. In many parts of the world—especially those with an oral tradition—the exchange of performances is an important trade item. (It is parallel to our practice of printing material as a means of exchanging ideas, scripts, techniques, etc.) Thus when Brook's group arrived they were greeted with requests for songs, dances, and plays. Brook describes the process exactly:

> We were just sitting and doing some improvised song, and the children asked us to come down to their little village, only a couple of miles away, because there was going to be some singing and dancing later in the night and everyone would be very pleased if we could come. So we said "sure." We walked down through the forest, found this village, and found that, indeed, there was a

ceremony going on. Somebody had just died and it was a funeral ceremony. We were made very welcome and we sat there, in total darkness under the trees, just seeing these moving shadows dancing and singing. And after a couple of hours they suddenly said to us: the boys say that this is what you do, too. Now you must sing for us. So we had to improvise a song for them. [11]

It is difficult but decisive to understand in these situations the relationship between what is the possession of one person and what belongs to the tribe (or group). In our romantic Western way we assume that it is in an either/or situation; but that is never so. Always an individual person possesses some esoteric and treasured information, technique, or thing: something which is done in his particular style, given his own shape or substance. The individual can trade this personal style to others; if the material is part of a sacred ceremony then certain regulations govern when and to whom it can be taught, and even how the instruction is relayed. At the same time the performance is "owned" it is the possession of the group because the "owner" thinks of himself as a repository, a library; and also because personal style is never altogether original but a new version of some traditional mode.

The interest in processions, parades, pilgrimages—movements through fairly large spaces arriving at performance centers, nodes of intense experience—is connected to the environmental idea. Although most environmental theatre (and all that is discussed in this book) takes place in enclosed and fixed spaces, there is a developing concept of working through the entire scale of a journey. Theatre touring is not a new idea, neither are religious pilgrimages. But these two occurrences may be converging. It may soon come about that theatres plan their tours not as discrete stops at prearranged places but as journeys through an area, stopping either where performances have been prearranged (as in the medieval cycle plays where the pageant wagons were drawn up to specific stations that further reverberated the themes of the play) or making unscheduled stops when special occasions arise, as with Brook's troupe in the African forest.

Victor Turner views the pilgrimage as a very special kind of human experience, one which I see closely connected to environmental theatre and the articulation not only of fixed spaces but of entire territories experienced not with a comprehensive birds-eye view but as an unfolding dramatic experience culminating in arrival and achieving a calm in the retreat.

> I tend to see pilgrimage as that form of institutionalized or symbolic anti-structure (or perhaps meta-structure) which succeeds the major initiation rites of puberty in tribal societies as the dominant historical form. It is the ordered anti-structure of patrimonial feudal systems. It is infused with voluntariness though by no means independent of structural obligatoriness. Its limen is much longer than that of initiation rites (in the sense that a long journey to a most sacred place used to take many months or years), and it breeds new types of secular liminality and communitas. [12]

Turner is saying that pilgrimages break down fixed social barriers, bringing people together in a community of those who are seeking the goal of the pilgrimage. In religious communities most pilgrimages are to known shrines (though there is also the life of the total pilgrimage, the permanent beggar-priest, always on the road). There is in contemporary theatre, just beginning now but I think destined to have an important future, the idea of using the tour, the trip, the journey with an unknown itinerary (using again time instead of space as the boundary and map) a means of extending the exploration of rehearsal into an actual realm of space. This is an extension of environmental staging to a new phase of understanding space, a more authentically global grasp of space. It makes all the world a stage, if not everyone in it actors.

Grotowski's most recent experiment, *The Fire on the Mountain*, is a similar work. In June-July 1975, Grotowski invited a number of people each to head a section of this work. Each person was asked to say exactly how he or she wanted to organize a group of people. Each group was domiciled on the mountain—not at its base but not at its summit either. On top of the mountain is a fire (what this means I don't know, except when I spoke with Grotowski he insisted that he meant the fire literally—not metaphorically). The spatial scheme looks like this:

Participants leave base
camps, ascend mountain,
meet others, descend to
camps. Cycle is repeated
many times over a period
of several days.

MAP OF GROTOWSKI'S
<u>FIRE ON THE MOUNTAIN</u>

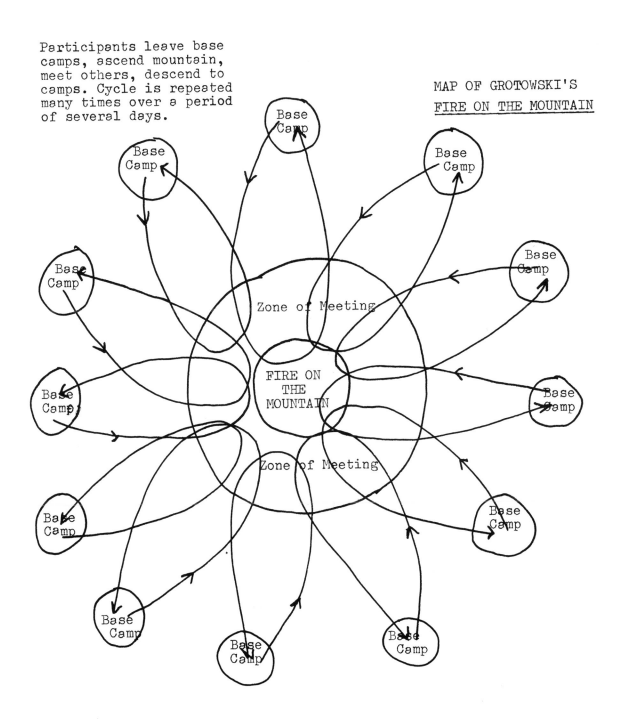

From each base camp at non-fixed intervals people ascend the mountain to the fire where they meet others coming from other base camps. On the top of the mountain interaction takes place, but this interaction is not fixed or pre-arranged—it is liminal and done in communitas (to use Turner's terms). Then individuals return to their camps. The process of ascending the mountain, meeting others, interacting (or not interacting), returning to camp continues for an undefined amount of time. The event is personal and collective; it is a pilgrimage in a double sense: getting to Poland to participate (or, if you are Polish, getting to the mountain); ascending-descending to and from the fire. Grotowski set a maximum of 1,000 total participants.*

The Living Theatre's most recent work, *Six Public Acts*, is also a pilgrimage. As I saw it in Ann Arbor, Michigan in May, 1975 at the second Invitational Festival of Experimental Theatre, it took place in six different locations both on and off the University of Michigan campus. Beginning in the Waterman Field House where an audience of about 1,500 assembled, it moved in steps to outside the engineering building, to the campus flagpole (a memorial for soldiers), a local bank, the main administration building, the ROTC building, and a new arts complex. At each of these sites an event was performed—such as the plague scene from *Mysteries* (at the engineering building), worship of a golden calf (at the bank), a "blood ritual" at the flagpole. The route of the performance, which took more than five hours, was:

---

*My description of *Fire on the Mountain* is based on a discussion I had with Grotowski two months before the event actually occurred. To see how the piece turned out, read Richard Mennen's "Jerzy Grotowski's Paratheatrical Projects" in TDR, Volume 19, Number 4, December 1975.

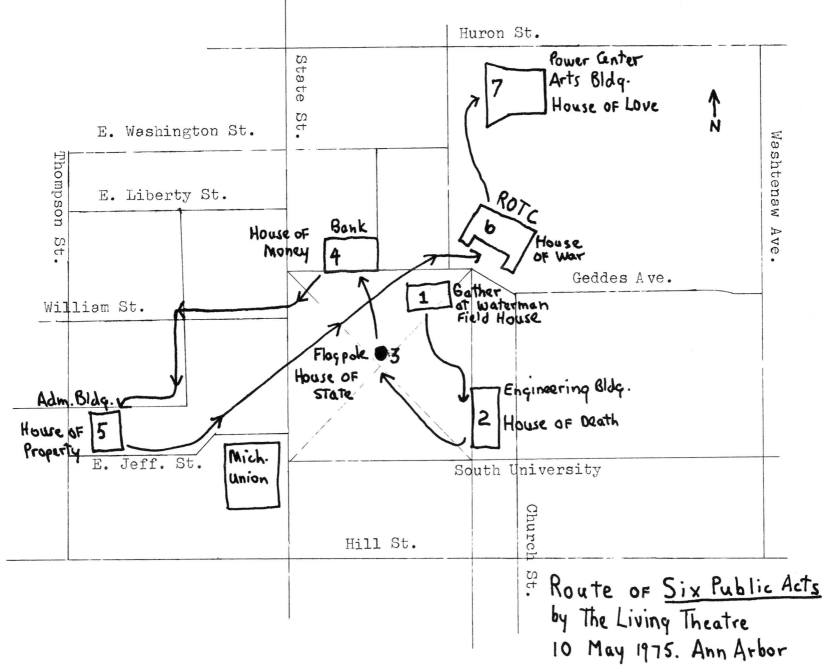

Huron St.

Power Center
Arts Bldg.
House of Love

7

N

E. Washington St.

State St.

Washtenaw Ave.

E. Liberty St.

Thompson St.

ROTC

House of
Money

Bank

4

6

House
of War

William St.

Geddes Ave.

1

Gather
at waterman
Field House

Flagpole ●3
House of
State

Adm. Bldg.

Engineering Bldg.

House of
Property

5

2

House of Death

E. Jeff. St.

Mich.
Union

South University

Church St.

Hill St.

Route of Six Public Acts
by The Living Theatre
10 May 1975. Ann Arbor

33

Each place it is performed it has a different route but with the same kinds of stopping places. I was disappointed in some of the activities—it was a piece in which the conception outran its execution (so much of what the Living did were repetitions or variations on images from their own earlier work); but the underlying concept of *Six Public Acts* was very precise: an articulation of a system of spaces, relating this landscape—this politically active topography—to the lives of the people living in it. It is very similar to what the Aborigines do to their lands in Australia. The difference is that for the most part the Living took a protestors' stance in relation to the land—they felt alien and expressed their hurt and anger that the land was being used to kill and exploit; the Aborigines feel love for their land and use their journeys as a form of worship, literally living through their ancestral myths.[13]

These recent performances are the latest development of environmental theatre. They connect to the themes I've discussed. They are non-mediated experiences that bring people out "into the field," where direct contact is made with the environment; and where person-to-person interaction is facilitated. In a way these theatre pieces use some of the lessons of the media against the media. The world is quite plainly more global today than it was 15 years ago it is possible to conceive of a single world-system. But at the same time such a unity makes us cherish ever more dearly person-to-person interaction on a small-scale, even intimate level. But this kind of interaction is not private. It is both intimate and public: a theatricalization (or ritualizing) of intimacy and interpersonal contact. Previously the audience watched such actions—the subject of theatre was the presentation of intimate acts in public and professionals were hired to perform these acts. Now often enough the audience is invited to originate or share in these acts. It is not participation in the drama (as in the 60's) but participation in

the act of making the theatrical event—a literal "come along and do it with us" that characterizes the most recent work of Brook, the Living, and Grotowski.

My own work is tempted in that direction but I am not there yet, if ever. A deep skepticism about religious experience, and the trap it lays for human expectations, the betrayals down the road of any utopian dream, keeps me back. My work has moved in the direction outlined in this book—a much more traditional direction. I stage plays using full spaces—but basically interior spaces (the outdoor scenes in *Mother Courage* work because they are placed against a production that takes place in the Garage). And, interested as I am in rituals, I don't stage them, I stage plays in which there are some ritual elements, some release into the communitas Turner feels is at the heart of all social solidarity.

In this book Rojo, McNamara, and I speak implicitly and explicitly about "them" and "us," about "orthodox," "traditional," "experimental," "environmental" and other theatrical terms that are slippery. I feel the divisions are not easy to locate because they can't be located on a strictly "what kind of theatre do you build" basis. For example, *Candide* as designed by Eugene Lee at the Chelsea Theatre Center of the Brooklyn Academy was an "us" production. It used full space, it had the audience constantly shifting its attention, it pressed the event in on them. Although the performance glowed with reflected not incandescent light (it was commercial even at BAM), that could be overlooked.

But when *Candide* moved to Broadway, its seating capacity multiplied, its ticket prices in heaven, its environment nailed down at every corner, its acting brassed-up to that shrill hilarity Broadway calls style—well, it was definitely "them." On the other hand, though Richard Foreman uses tunnel staging, putting his audience on the far side of a space divided in two by a more-than-symbolic string; though he hasn't even hinted audience participation; though he controls every aspect of his production preferring to work with untrained performers—his work is a resounding "us." Why? Because he thinks of space— he designs himself every inch of the space of his theatre, the space the performance is in, the space the audience is in; he crafts every detail of the production and he doesn't think of the theatre either as a "realization of text" or as a conglomeration of independent "theatre arts." He looks at his work as a unity; he rethinks his whole process for each production. In short, his theatre is his, not manipulated by those who use theatre to make a buck. He is interested in expanding and changing the consciousness of his audience; he respects them and exploits neither performers nor spectators.

The term "orthodox" also needs a glossary. I use the term where others might prefer "traditional." But I am sharply aware that environmental theatre is traditional—if you consider the tradition of Greek, medieval, and early Renaissance theatre; if you consider the many oral cultures still existing. I believe some streams of the current dominant theatre—commercial, regional, academic—are cancerous and therefore dangerous, deserving to be destroyed. The term "orthodox" suggests a rigidity, stubborness, inertia, and stupidity which I find in the commercial theatre that takes all art as "property" (not to be traded as in Australia or Africa but to be capitalized), to those regional theatres that see their job as pleasing the drugged consciousnesses of the middle classes; to those university theatres that build monster art centers so burdened with equipment that their students lose all touch of the art of making (which is, after all, what poetry and performance are all about). These fossils still reign from their banks and their museums. They corrupt the young. I do not offer them hemlock, but I don't wish them luck either.

[1] Among the growing literature of and on guerrilla theatre I recommend Karen Malpede Taylor, *People's Theatre in Amerika* (Drama Book Specialists, 1974), Arthur Sainer, *Radical Theatre Notebook* (Avon, 1975), and Henry Lesnick, editor, *Guerrilla Theatre* (Avon, 1973). Ironically, Avon is a subsidiary of the Hearst Corporation.

[2] Robert Brustein, "News Theater," *New York Times Magazine*, June 16, 1974, p. 7.

[3] See Ronnie Davis, "Guerrilla Theatre," TDR (T-32), 1966, 130-136.

[4] Cage in an "Interview with John Cage," TDR (T-32), 1965, 50.

[5] Goffman, *Presentation of Self in Everyday Life* (NY: Anchor, 1959), 72.

[6] See TDR (T-58, T-65) for features on New and Postmodern Dance.

[7] See Michael Kirby's, "The New Theatre," a definitive essay on the theory of happenings. TDR (T-30), 23-43. Also included in Kirby's *The Art of Time*.

[8] Oldenburg, *Store Days* (New York: Something Else Press, 1967), 39.

[9] For an analysis of the impact of non-Western performance on our own theatre see my essays: "Actuals" (Theatre Quarterly, No. 2, 1971), 49-66; and "From Ritual to Theatre and Back" (ETJ, December 1974), 455-481.

[10] Slater, Earthwalk (New York: Anchor), 58.

[11] Brook, "Brook's Africa," TDR (T-59, 1973), 45.

[12] Turner, *Dramas, Fields, and Metaphors* (Ithaca: Cornell University Press, 1974), 182.

[13] For an account of the Aboriginal experience see Richard A. Gould, *Yiwara* (New York: Scribners, 1969).

Transforming Existing Spaces: Fixed Environments

1 Sarah Lawrence College

In December of 1969, Jerry Rojo began work for Wilford Leach on designs for an experimental theatre at Sarah Lawrence College in Bronxville, New York. The theatre, completed in 1974, is part of a performing-arts complex designed by George Yourke of the architectural firm of Warner-Burns-Toan-Lunde in New York City. The space used for the experimental theatre is the stage house of the former college auditorium, essentially a multi-purpose room which may be organized to create either an arena or an end-stage, and designed to house productions employing minimal scenery. Basically, however, the Sarah Lawrence Theatre is a fixed, permanent environment made up of wooden platforms, small stages, galleries, and staircases—all of which may be used either by actors or spectators. The audience capacity ranges from 125 to 200, depending upon the way in which the room is used for production. There is no fixed seating.

BMc: Who did you do the project for?

JR: Will Leach, the artistic director at Sarah Lawrence. Leach is a designer himself. He was trying to find a system that would allow him to create a performance space in the stage house of a proscenium theatre. The auditorium was turned over to the music department.

BMc: Can you describe your earliest solutions to the problems of that stage house?

JR: The early ones were rather like my *Makbeth* environment which I did with The Performance Group in 1969. I designed a series of fairly large playing areas throughout the space. There was one large center performance area, but there were also others comparable in size in different parts of the room. I presented the design to Will who was opposed to it because he wanted a stage situated in a single place. His own work was end-stage oriented.

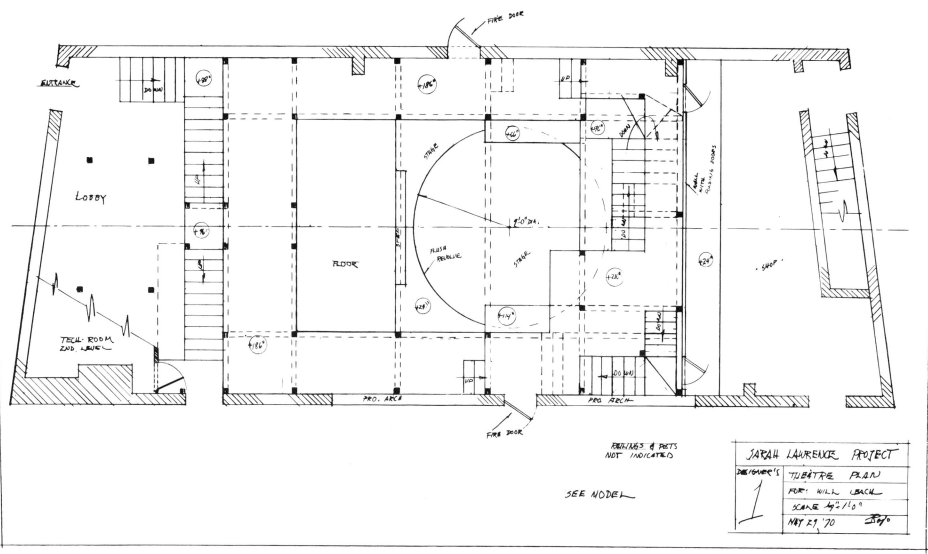

ENTRANCE

LOBBY

TECH·ROOM
2ND·LEVEL

FLOOR

STAGE

STAGE

FLUSH
REVOLVE

9'0" DIA.

SHOP

FIRE DOOR

FIRE DOOR

PRO. ARCH

PRO. ARCH

WALL WITH FOLDING DOORS

DOWN

DOWN

UP

UP

UP

DOWN

+88"

+186"

+186"

+8"

+29"

+114"

+66"

+96"

+24"

+24"

RAILINGS & POSTS
NOT INDICATED

SEE MODEL

SARAH LAWRENCE PROJECT
DESIGNER'S
THEATRE PLAN
FOR: WILL LEACH
SCALE ⅜"=1'0"
MAY 29 '70   Rojo

Ground plan of Sarah Lawrence Project by Jerry Rojo.

BMc: Will you describe the solution at which you ultimately arrived?

JR: The idea was to develop a unified theatre, where the acting areas, the audience areas, the shop areas could be contained in one room. We were interested in pursuing a totally open-space theatre: when the audience comes in, they see the entire space; there is a feeling that they are privy to everything that is going on. As you come into the theatre, you see the lobby area and you're in the midst of posts and stairs leading to the second and third galleries, and the tech booth above them. You stand in the lobby and look all the way through the performing areas into the shop because the whole theatre is an open timber structure. The galleries lead you toward a stage area with a revolve in it. Upstage of the revolve is a complex of stairs and balconies like an updated Elizabethan inner above-inner below which is directly accessible from the seating galleries. Directly behind the stage is the workshop. So that there always can be sufficient access from the workshop through the complex and onto the stage proper, this whole facade can be taken apart.

The space does not have fixed seating. I thought it was important that the students find uses for the entire space, even the lobby area. My instinct was to keep the space as open as possible, not to define it. If you look at the plan, the more ordered end of the theatre is the audience area; as you move toward the stage the shapes become more amorphous, and more interesting. What we wound up with, I think, is a blend of a traditional actor/audience relationship and an open-space performance area.

RS: The idea of seeing from the lobby area, to the audience area, to the playing area, to the shop, is extraordinary. The impulse of orthodox theatre people using this space may be to mask off the lobby and the shop. If they resist and allow their work to flow through so that whatever is happening in the shop can be felt in the playing area productions will have an extraordinary sense of actuality.

BMc: It recapitulates the whole history of the production.

RS: Yes, it reminds me of Copeau's Vieux Colombier where there is a fixed area at one end—permanent structure—and facing that a rather simple audience area. And, of course, the Copeau theatre is a transformation of the Elizabethan fixed space. The Sarah Lawrence Theatre is part of this tradition.

BMc: What materials did you use? And how does your use of materials relate to your solution?

JR: The right materials were very important to Will Leach. We talked about steel. I felt that we could do a great deal structurally with it and gain an open feeling at the same time. Will was against it. Finally we got around to wood. Its softness and the fact that it's an organic material were the predominant reasons why the theatre became a wood-beam structure.

RS: You tend to give good, rational reasons for choosing wood, but I think underneath is the plain fact that you love wood.

BMc: You always want to work in metal at some point, but the structures usually end up being wood. Once you said you were interested in engineering rather than stage design. Maybe wood is the perfect material for your kind of "engineering".

JR: I think there is also a "poor theatre" concept here. I like to go to ordinary places—the local lumber yard—and get materials that are immediately available. When people know

Designer's preliminary sketch by Jerry Rojo.

the materials being used they feel comfortable with them. I find it is a beautiful notion to make ingenious statements using commonplace things.

BMc: This is against the current direction in stagecraft which focuses on the use of materials like plastic and metal that are new to theatre.

RS: I also think that wood has great practical advantages. It's the most "cannibalizable" of materials. I know that in the Performing Garage, we're still using lumber that we first used in *Dionysus in 69,* some six years ago. In our time, when everything is thrown away, I like things that you use and change and reuse—things you artistically recycle.

JR: There's another practical reason for the use of wood in this project. This theatre will not have much, if any, scenery—essentially because it's an actors'/directors' theatre. Still, you can do anything you want to the wood because its a soft, malleable material. This space will be used up in a few years, nails will be pounded into it, pieces cut away. But it can also be replaced relatively easily.

Often the main problem with wooden structures is the building or fire codes. Every project we've done in wood has run up against regulations that say wood can't be used the way I want in a theatre or a room designed for public occupancy.

We've forced the inspectors or fire marshals to negotiate the problem. I've always felt—let's do it, and then let them deal with it. They can't tear the environment down, they have to find a solution. And that's what happened at Sarah Lawrence. We had to install a sprinkler system in this particular case. Then, by negotiating with the architect, the fire marshal, and the building inspector, we arrived at an acceptable theatre.

BMc: As it stands the building and fire codes make insufficient provision for the kind of work you're doing. That has to change.

RS: An interesting thing about working with an existing space like the stage house at Sarah Lawrence, is that you accept what you have. A lot of new theatres designed and built from scratch are bland because there has been no previous life in the space. You get something that is architecturally precise, with surfaces that are even or regular. But a space that someone has already been in for a long time has earned its lumps—it carries its history in it. I find this an advantage, because from a dialogue with an existing "personality"—a space that's been lived in—a theatre space takes it tensions. Completely designed spaces, from the Arena Stage in Washington to the Guthrie in Minneapolis, seem bland, regular, sterile, and deadening.

BMc: The Sarah Lawrence Theatre is a so-called "fixed" environment. What exactly do you mean by that?

JR: In a fixed environment like the Sarah Lawrence Theatre, or the Mobius Theatre, which we'll talk about later, the edges of space are predetermined, more or less. The entrances, levels, and structures are always in the same places. But a director and the performers can find ways to make the space over anew for each production. They transform the space. The place can take on an entirely new character for different productions.

RS: In post-Renaissance Western culture, we automatically think of "fixed" as meaning that the edges are fixed and the center flexible—you build in from a framed edge. I could conceive of a theatre where the center is fixed and what goes on around the edges is flexible. I don't think we have ever worked in a theatre, or designed one with a fixed center and edges that were flexible and transformational.

BMc: Except perhaps in the streets. A case in point would be a mountebank who sets up a booth in the street. He becomes the fixed center; the "auditorium" is freely defined by the people who gather in the street around his booth.

RS: I have a feeling that, to a certain degree, filmic space also has a fixed center, with a flexible edge. What is fixed in the filmic space is the camera itself, which is always the hub of the wheel; the edges of the wheel are what the camera sees. I think that the filmic idea can be applied to live performance. I want to set up a number of stage platforms on Wooster Street, outside our theatre, and move action from one to another—not exactly dollying, at least not in a technical sense, but it is close. For example: I want to do one scene where the audience goes outside on Wooster Street. We open the overhead rolling door of the theatre and behind is a little box set in a perfect proscenium. We play a scene there. Then, in the next scene, the audience goes inside and looks out through the door, and we play another scene down the street, perhaps moving around the corner. In a sense we will be building an environment the edges of which are constantly changing. What is fixed is our theatre, The Performing Garage, as center, as headquarters. Wherever the audience is would be the camera eye and center.

A really artistic environment is a function between a fixed point and a flexible set of points. Whether the fixed complex happens to be the walls and the ceilings of a room or in the center of a space doesn't make any difference. But I think there has to be negotiation between fixed and flexible. What's wrong with these multi-purpose theatres where everything is supposedly flexible, is that there's no center of attention. "Flexible" is a slippery concept but, on the other hand, I can't find anything exciting about a space where everything is fixed.

Designer's model for Sarah Lawrence Theatre by Jerry Rojo. From bottom to top of photo is the backstage area, the main environment area and the lobby/technical booth area. Photo: Bill Bixby

2 The Phoenix Bus

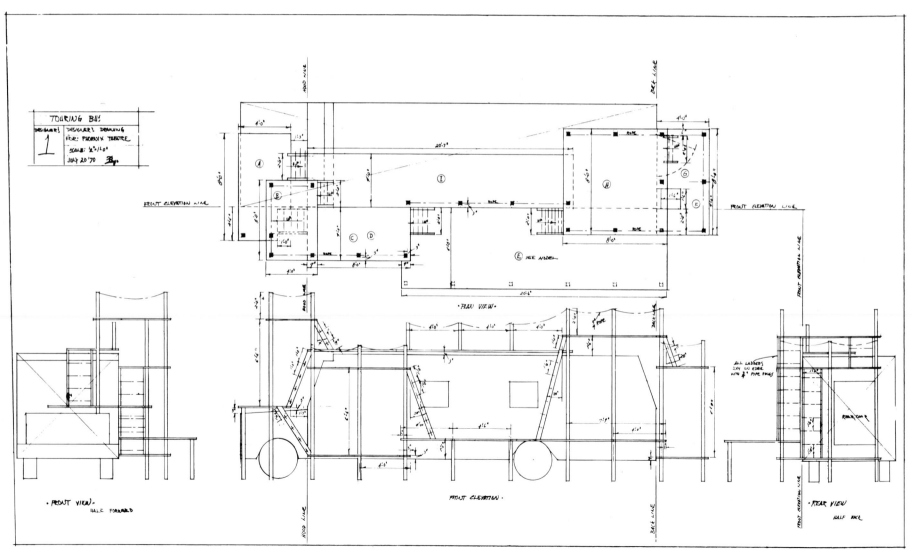

Designer's working drawings of The Phoenix Bus by Jerry Rojo.

The Phoenix Theatre Touring Bus was a multiple-stage complex on wheels used by a street theatre company associated with New York's Phoenix Theatre. The idea was conceived during the summer of 1970, and the complex was completed in the fall of that year, using as a base a 1967 GMC school bus. Designed by Jerry Rojo, with the assistance of technical director George Lindsay, the exterior of the bus was fitted out as a fixed environment made up of collapsible platforms, ladders, and stair units which fold onto the side of the vehicle or are stored inside during transit from one performance site to another. Hydraulic jacks are used to stabilize the bus during performance. Audiences stand or sit on one side of the bus, which is designed for use in streets, on playgrounds, or in virtually any other convenient outdoor space.

BMc: Who did you do the project for?

JR: For Gordon Duffy, who was operating a street theatre project for the Phoenix Theatre.

BMc: Can you describe their bus and tell me how they proposed to use it?

JR: The bus was relatively new and in very good condition. I think it orginally seated about 40 people. But they'd taken all the seats out, and the idea was to use the bus as a kind of touring stage. So they asked me to develop a performance complex out of it—a complex, incidentally, that would conform to motor vehicle regulations which required that the head and tail lights be visible and placed height and width restrictions for road use. The complex was not designed for the performers to live in: it was a moving theatre. The idea was to make it self-contained with light and sound equipment, and all the necessary technology. It was a kind of multi-level moving stagehouse, made up of a series of stages connected by ladders. We were trying to develop all the possiblities of the bus given a certain budget and the motor vehicle codes, which restricted the road-ready bus, by requiring the stages to fold to 16' by 8'.

BMc: What materials did you use to create these levels?

JR: We used steel for the framing members and plywood for surface material. Because the stages were welded to the bus, we didn't need angle bracing. We just lowered them and rested them on vertical supports. These vertical supports were 4" by 4" wooden posts with pins. It was really a simple solution: the stages folded up onto the sides of the bus and the vertical supports were stored in the bus. All of this had to stay within the length of the bus and motor vehicle height limitations. We used the wood, pipe, and steel naturally, without going into any kind of color.

BMc: What lighting instruments did you carry and how were they used on the bus?

JR: That was an interesting problem. We had to draw power locally. We couldn't depend on getting high voltage; we had to stay within 120 volts. So the system was adapted for going into a drugstore and plugging into their outlets, which, I think, is a kind of interesting alternative to running cable all over the place. For the most part, however, the bus was a daytime open-air operation. They didn't use much lighting equipment; they used daylight and sunlight.

BMc: In what kind of spaces did they set up the bus?

JR: Well, for example, they did one of their pieces at 33 Wooster Street, parked in the street right in front of The Performing Garage. The bus was designed so that it could be adjusted to the crown in the road, with jacks.

BMc: What was the flow of space on the bus?

JR: I wanted to make it, inside and out, a total, flowing environment. I thought of the bus windows, for example, as places for little plays to take place and as little entrances for the performers. There was a fairly large level or platform in the front, which was accessible both to other platforms on the side and to the roof. There was really a flow from the front of the bus, up to the top, and on to the street proper, so that actors could move down into the audience and back up again.

RS: This is an example of the kind of space I was talking of earlier. The center—the school bus—is fixed: You have wheels, axles, motor, the basic shape. Jerry built out from that center and established edges. Then events were performed on and around it creating other indeterminate edges. I think the bus presents a contrast to a project like Sarah Lawrence, where the edges are fixed and the center is what's reconstructed.

RS: In outdoor events like this, the event attracts an audience around it, because the event is special. In the regular indoor theatrical situation, however, you come inside something; you are forced to move towards the center because there are fixed boundaries.

BMc: Are you saying that this kind of outdoor event is centrifugal?

RS: Yes. It seems to me that when you're inside a space, you get a psychologically moving experience, an experience where you can be swept away, but outdoors it's a more remote experience, because at any moment you know you can leave. The further away you get, the less the event means; the closer you get, the more you are drawn into it. When you enter an environmental space where the walls contain you, you're in a "heated" environment. For example, in initiation ceremonies, there are almost always huts, or enclosed spaces, where some of the ceremonies take place secretly. In these spaces highly charged, heated experiences take place—some of the most secret and violent of the rites. But the celebrations that follow these rites are in open spaces which have a different quality—where people come, gather, and go away again.

BMc: We're talking about a festival idea of theatre which draws a "flexible" crowd, a crowd that participates in the event much more loosely than in an enclosed space.

RS: Right. A festival theatre has a heated center, but the event gets weaker on the periphery.

BMc: There's a different kind of transaction between the space and the performance going on in each of those two models. In the festival model, we're talking about a performance which often tends to be very large in scale. Medieval passion plays or the Macy's parade are broadly done, not played out in the kind of minute detail that is typical of the event presented in a confined and specific space.

It seems to me that the Phoenix Bus owes more to the festival model, to popular forms, than it does to orthodox theatre structures and orthodox theatre scenography.

RS: We're talking about scenography as a product of social and political as well as esthetic ideas. In street theatre, guerrilla theatre, campesino theatre, and so on, the theatrical event is developed from below rather than from above. In the 18th and 19th centuries, theatre got more and more bourgeois until the rise of Marxism. During the last 50 years, there has been a welling up from the popular arts: sports, TV, film, street action and other popular forms.

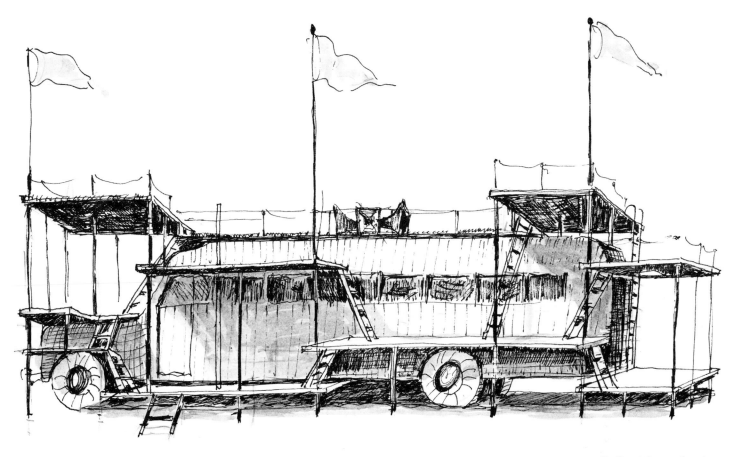

The Phoenix Bus set up for action.

𝟛 The College of White Plains

The reception lounge at The College of White Plains before renovation. Photo: Bruce Wolf

In 1971, the College of White Plains, a New York women's college, assigned its Director of Theatre, Beverly Brumm, a space consisting of a dormitory, a large lounge, and a number of adjoining rooms which were to be remodeled as a performance center. Designed by Jerry Rojo and Brooks McNamara, with Edmund Seagrave, and with Jerry Powell as technical director, the remodeled lounge became an open space theatre, without fixed seating or a permanent stage, which can accommodate a wide variety of actor/audience relationships. The new theatre, which holds 250 spectators, can easily be adapted for end-stage, arena, thrust, corner-stage, and various forms of environmental productions. In essence, it is what is known as a "black box" theatre. Although the theatre is on the ground floor of an occupied dormitory, it was readily approved for public occupancy, in part because orthodox stage scenery was not used in the room. Instead, a number of movable fireproofed panels were built which can be used to organize space in virtually any way required for production.

BMc: The theatre at the College of White Plains was made from a room about 50' by 60', which had formerly been a parlor in a women's dormitory. An arcade runs along two sides. There is a relatively low ceiling, about 12' high, a fireplace at one end, and exits into other rooms—into a corridor in one case, into a small anteroom in another. We had the use of several adjoining rooms, one of which was converted to a lighting booth.

JR: Our idea was to set up an open space theatre with the "working" area on the ceiling and the walls. Essentially, the floor was kept open for the performers and the structures needed for each new production, while walls and ceiling were what Richard calls "hot." Specifically, we developed a grid area for suspending lightweight scenery and lights. The grid contained a number of outlets—about 50 outlets led into a

Renovation of the lounge area in progress. Photo: Beverly Brumm

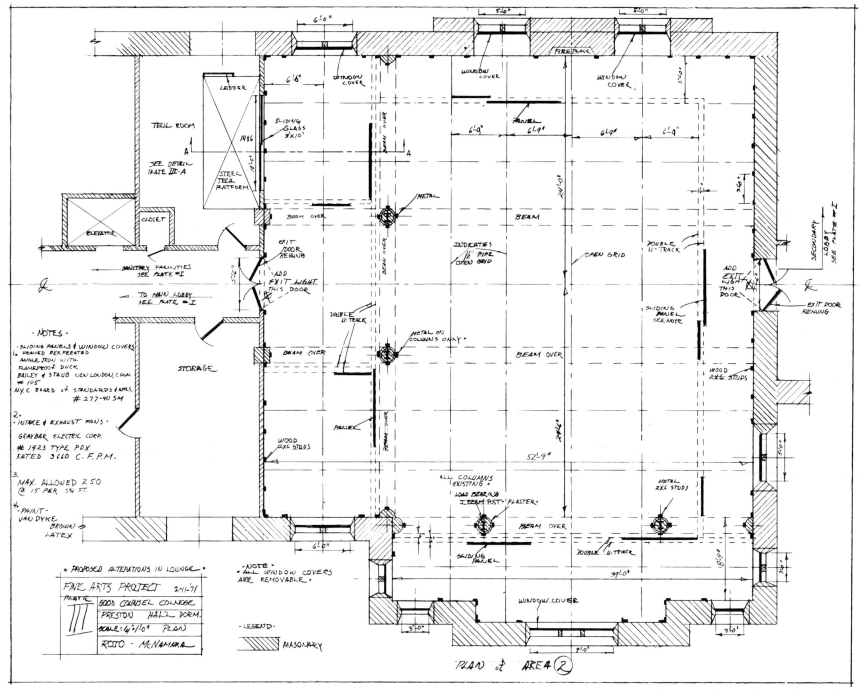

Ground plan of the theatre after renovations. Jerry Rojo.

lighting booth where the dimmer system was located.

BMc: Also on the grid was a track system that ran around three sides of the room, in front of the two arcades, and along the side opposite the longer of the two. From that track were suspended panels constructed of aluminum, covered with canvas. The panels could be bolted together through the aluminum framing. They were hung on the track to form corridors around the center of the room, with gaps to create doors through which actors could enter and exit. The panels could also be taken down, joined and set up like screens in other places in the room. Frequently, they were used in conjunction with a set of modular platform units which could be formed into corner stages, irregular arena stages, irregular thrust stages, and so on.

JR: The walls were masonry, very difficult to work on, so we came up with the idea of putting 2″ by 6″ studs on 3′ centers, anchored into the walls very securely, so that platforms could be built off them and people could hang from them. All four walls in the room have an "epiderm," a skin on which scenic problems can be worked out.

It's traditional when audience and performers share the same space to try to make the room invisible. We didn't want that and we didn't want to have a white room; we wanted to maintain the basic color of the room—that of the black walnut woodwork.

BMc: So we went to a Van Dyke brown, a very dark brown. That created neutrality, but still worked with the Renaissance architectural features—the fireplace, the colonnades, and so on—which were intact. This is an idea we were talking about earlier. We were not interested in negating the previous use of the space when we adapted it to a theatre by creating a black

hole. We wanted to keep the integrity of that space and to adapt the best features of it for performance.

RS: I think there's something else involved in that, too. While black space can be exhilarating for some audiences, it can also be threatening. The all-black room has associations with darkness and foreboding. A white room has associations of sterility, medicine, and so on.

BMc: How would you contrast the potential flow of performance in this room with that of the earlier project at Sarah Lawrence?

JR: Here at White Plains, the room is entirely open to structures, and to any kind of actor/audience relationship. It could be purely environmental: You could do a street theatre piece, or you could structure arena productions. The room has, because of the interesting colonnades, a strong corner on which the director might want to focus. But essentially it is flexible. I should add that the shape of the room means that you must have horizontal action almost entirely, because you cannot really get off the floor more than about 6′. Whereas with the Sarah Lawrence project's 25′ ceiling we were really able to deal with vertical space.

4 The Mobius Theatre

The Mobius Theatre at the University of Connecticut grew out of the Sarah Lawrence project. Since 1961, Jerry Rojo has been a faculty member at Connecticut; in 1970, Rojo approached the then head of the theatre department, David Heilweil, with a concept for an environmental theatre incorporating ideas from his designs for The Performance Group's *Makbeth*. The Mobius Theatre, under the technical direction of Robert McCaw and architect/advisor Richard Swibold, was completed in the fall of 1971. It was set up in what had previously been an arena, and was designed to be a fixed environment of platforms, stairs and companionways. The environment, which has no fixed audience seating, allows the production concept to determine actor/spectator relationships: by manipulation of the audience it is possible to set up an end-stage, an arena, a thrust, or an environmental situation. In 1973 Rojo developed an environmental theatre training program at the University of Connecticut, using the Mobius Theatre to conduct workshops which culminated in three productions, *Baal Games*, *Our House*, and *The Big Enchilada*.

BMc: What did you want to do at the Mobius?

JR: I wanted to develop something like the *Makbeth* environment at The Performing Garage—a space filled with large "stations" that could serve as performance islands throughout the room.

BMc: In what kind of space was the Mobius Theatre created?

JR: The space, in the Fine Arts complex, is separated from a studio theatre by tall double doors. The studio theatre is a small proscenium house seating about 100 people. The room which became the Mobius was originally used for arena productions. It contained portable seating and a riser system and was 38′ square and 22′ high. Because of student labor, the Mobius Theatre only

cost $6,000 to build and by the time we had used it for two years and five productions, it had paid for itself.

BMc: Explain your solution to the problems of the room.

JR: I was trying to develop a fixed environment—an environment that filled the whole room—on the theory that any production can be dealt with environmentally. I feel that Chekhov, Ibsen—any play, in fact—can be presented in a fixed environment. However, the theatre can be used, if one chooses to, as an arena or an end-stage or an Elizabethan thrust stage.

BMc: You mean by simply creating focus at a particular point in the space? You're saying that the room itself makes no "statement" in the direction of a particular style or a particular period, that anything is possible within it?

RS: Any text is adaptable to environmental production. Let me give you an example. Obviously Shakespeare's plays were not written for the proscenium, but they have been done in the proscenium. Ditto for the Greeks. Any theatrical space can accommodate any text, because a text is an abstraction and a space is a concretization. It's not that the space doesn't make a statement—it definitely does—but the play text doesn't make an unalterable statement about space. That's an argument that I would stick to: no play text makes any limiting statement about space. All you can say is that historically it has been done in such and such a space. A spatial analysis of a given text will yield many possibilities—all of which say more about who is doing the play than about the play itself. In fact, the play itself doesn't exist—only versions of its possibilities.

BMc: Actually, every historical period redefines the space supposedly appropriate to a classic play. We constantly reconstruct plays in our own image.

Detail photograph of the designer's model
of The Mobius Theatre. Model by Jerry Rojo.
Photo: Bill Bixby

JR: I think it is essential that anybody building a theatre, whatever kind of theatre, allows it to have potential for vertical and diagonal action, as well as horizontal action. Not that life goes up, necessarily, but only that action wants to go up. Position in space is very important, because life is so much involved with these positions. A strictly horizontal room seems to me to undermine life's action, and thus limits the director and the performers.

BMc: And yet, verticality in the theatre has not been explored. Most frequently the emphasis is horizontal.

JR: In the proscenium theatre, they've never dealt with that space above the audience's heads. And that's a criminally wasted space, it seems to me. So in theatres like the Mobius I want to force a total use of the space—at last. If you force the production into a room that has a vertical sense to it, you have to use it. The production is obligated to deal with it.

For student projects done in studio theatres, the tradition is a small proscenium stage with blocks to simulate furniture, or screens and panels to divide the space. All of this limits the action to the horizontal plane. Any vertical or cubic use of the space is discouraged—partly because it is too costly to build scenic elements. The idea of the Mobius was to force students and directors to deal with the vertical space—because it was there and because it is fixed and cannot be removed. It has worked. The directing and acting classes have been reoriented so that they are getting away from the living room-realistic Method acting style, and becoming more conscious of time and space. It is a training program that leads students to deal with extremes and once you have come to control them, then it is possible to limit yourself to the horizontal—if you have to.

BMc: Will you describe what was done to the space that became the Mobius Theatre?

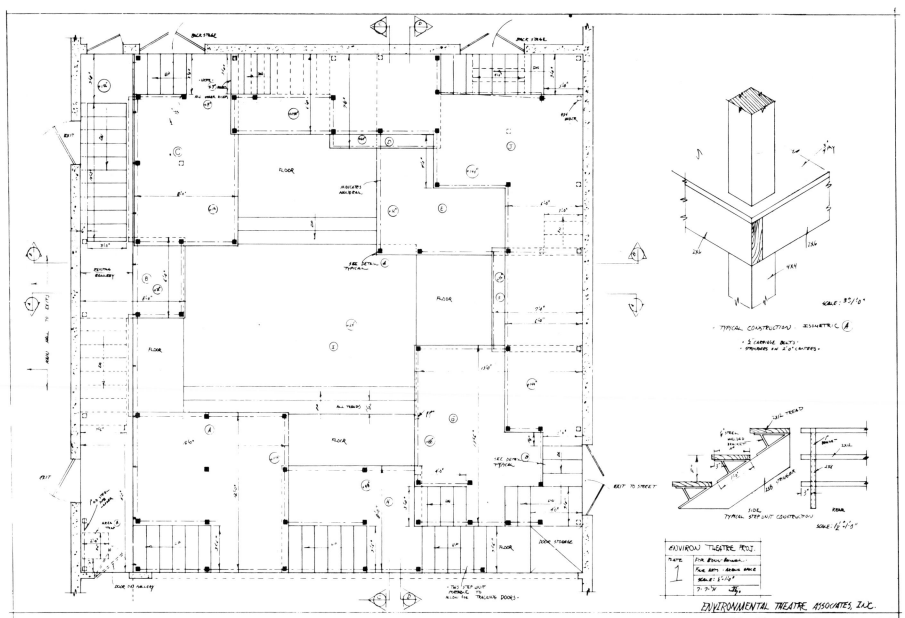

Ground plan of The Mobius environment by Jerry Rojo.

JR: In the Performing Garage we've used ladders, ramps, and ship's ladders—many different methods of access. In the Mobius, the attempt was more orthodox. It was the same concept that one would find in a building—stairs and stairwells, steps and landings. Circumscribing the entire room are the stairwells and the landings. When you come to a landing, you can stop and look toward the center of the room and then move into a gallery or a stairwell, and on to other spaces. Basically the room is circled with galleries. Protruding from those at the corners are large playing areas. The corners are pointing into the room; there are four of them and in the middle is a central playing area. It is a portable stage and it is the only part of the room that can be shifted. It's designed to break away, so that the whole floor can be left open to allow for the possibility of using television or motion picture cameras, or for use as a dance floor.

BMc: Presumably you could put an audience there and have action take place around the galleries.

JR: Right.

BMc: Can you tell me something about the materials that were used?

JR: Vertical supports, 4" by 4" construction supports for framing, 2" by 6" for construction, 3/4" plywood for surface materials, 3/4" plate for hand rails with a speed rail kind of fitting, which is fundamentally a set screw.

BMc: As in the Sarah Lawrence project, you seem to stick primarily to wood. Why?

JR: I think it's just because I like wood. It's an economical material—at least it used to be. We're trained to use wood before we're trained to use any other kind of material.

BMc: This also seems to be linked with your use of color—or in fact, your use of no color within the environment. It seems that in the Sarah Lawrence environment and here as well, there is relatively little color. There is natural wood, and raw metal, but very few direct color statements. Why?

JR: Except for attempting to take color out of something, to neutralize, I do relatively little. I feel that color is a private thing and belongs to the people who inhabit an environment. The other thing I find is that the natural grain of wood is very beautiful in itself.

BMc: It's interesting that you use extreme scenic complexity and no color complexity at all. Is there no possibility of you ever reversing that, of working with intense color complexity and a simple architecture?

JR: I think I can organize space architecturally; that's what I've trained myself to do. I enjoy going into a room and doing something to it in a literal, physical sense. I think you can play games with color—you can play games with space too, for that matter—but there's a very satisfying concreteness about the development of space. A human being who enters it has to stand here, he has to go from here to there. It's very direct. Color, I find, is very private and psychological.

RS: You can say about color what John Cage says about sound: It's always there. What you're talking about is not color versus colorlessness, but about different uses of color. It's like white light as opposed to filtered light. There's a habit in the American theatre of colored light. This habit is connected to illusionism and indoor spaces. Sunlight is anti-illusionistic; it is white and clear. There's an association of white light with the outdoors and the workaday. The "magic" world is technicolor, filtered. The workaday world is anti-technicolor, anti-illusionistic. In white

The *Big Enchilada* in performance at The Mobius Theatre, 1975. Clockwise, Linford Carey, Dennis Prueher, Phyllis Robinson and Elyse Greenhut. Directed by Jerry Rojo. Photo: Alan Decker.

light the focus is on the audience, on the architectural configuration of the space, on the event. Color blurs the event, covers up the performance, and makes the space disappear into what it appears to be.

BMc: How would you compare the relationship of audience to actor to space—the flow of performance—between the Mobius Theatre, The Good Council project, and The Sarah Lawrence project?

JR: The most obvious thing in this theatre is that the audience literally uses the same space that the performers use. In a given production, they both have to occupy the same space; they both must use the same stairwells. It's possible to have the audience not use certain areas, but that goes against the grain of the theatre.

BMc: Is this also true of the Sarah Lawrence project?

JR: No, it's not. You see, at Sarah Lawrence it's possible to have the audience concentrated at one end. In the Mobius, when you come in, you're into the theatre—it's a sort of cold-turkey theatre. At Sarah Lawrence, you can work your way down to one end, away from the performance. But here, you have no choice, you're immediately in it.

RS: There's a feature here that connects to Meyerhold's idea of a theatre being a theatre. When I'm in the Mobius, I'm aware that I'm in that theatre. I don't forget the space I'm in, nor do I ever think of it as anything except the space that it is. If I go to a theatre with an illusionistic production style, part of the work of the scenery is to make me forget about the space I'm sitting in and concentrate on the second space on stage.

JR: Let me say further that the space encourages acting and directing that is very physical. In the Mobius, I have developed a style of environmental performance that emphasizes the actor's body in real time and space with few if any props or costumes. I think that this kind of theatre architecture teaches and fosters organic, living theatre which has no historical precedents or models. Whereas, matrix-oriented orthodox theatre is based on imitation of historical images and ideas for both design and direction.

BMc: Where exactly does the audience sit in the Mobius? And how does their location relate to the places occupied by the performers?

JR: The seating is determined by the production. But there are many possibilities. For example, each member of the audience may get a little square of carpet on which he can sit. The squares have double-edge tape surfaces so they can be placed and picked up and moved about very easily. Then, there are benches around the space. These give people a more conventional kind of seating; but they also help make good use of the space because they offer sightlines down into the space. Then, there are people who move about the space at will. To see something under one of the platforms, for example, you might have to go up into a gallery opposite, or climb up on top of another platform. You literally approach the event itself.

Rehearsal in progress of *Our House* in The Mobius Theatre, 1974. Photo: Mike Duffy

5 The University of Connecticut Inner Auditorium

The Albert Jorgensen Auditorium at the University of Connecticut is the school's main concert hall, seating some 4,000 spectators. During 1970 and 1971, Jerry Rojo, with Edmund Seagrave as technical director, completed an "inner auditorium" seating 700 which may be set up inside the main concert hall when a smaller house is desired. The inner auditorium consists of a three-quarter round seating area with a thrust stage and a sound shell. The entire seating and stage area is composed of a riser system that easily folds onto carts which are rolled into an adjacent room for storage. Later changes in the space have also made it possible to seat 500 or 1,200 in two frontal seating arrangements.

BMc: The inner auditorium at the University of Connecticut. Who did you do the project for?

JR: It was done for the Albert Jorgensen Auditorium at the University of Connecticut which handles the major concert series on campus. Michael Brotman is the managing director. The University was interested in attempting to develop a smaller, inner theatre within the Auditorium so that they could do one-man shows and small-scale intimate concerts. In the past, string quartets, say, would have to go to another hall, and Brotman wanted to have everything unified within a single space.

BMc: So that the original 4,000-seat Auditorium had to remain essentially intact and you had to float a new theatre inside it. Will you describe the Auditorium?

JR: Behind the proscenium arch is the traditional sort of stage house for a concert hall—complete with a band shell. The proscenium opening is about 80' wide and 30' high. The stage is fairly shallow. The main floor of the Auditorium is a totally open flat floor—a fact which is important in this case.

The floor was surrounded by a horseshoe gallery on three sides, with fixed seating. At the back of the Auditorium are a second and third balcony. It's a very high room, probably 60' to the ceiling. For each major concert series portable seats were set on the flat floor. These would be taken down for dances, exhibitions, and other large-scale events.

BMc: What were your earliest solutions to the problem of putting an inner auditorium in this space?

JR: The main problems were the flat floor and the vast space. The spectator was lost in the midst of a sea of people, all seated at the same level. To eliminate this problem, and to set them into closer contact with the stage, we wanted risers for the audience.

I felt that whatever I did had to be in keeping with the existing space. I tried to work with materials like those already there so that someone coming into the inner auditorium, not having seen it previously, would think that it had always been there.

BMc: Were you interested in blocking off the inner theatre from the rest of the main floor space with walls or baffles of any kind?

JR: No. The inner auditorium is really a part of the total space.

BMc: Did you use the entire ground floor space for the inner auditorium?

JR: No. We used the edges of the gallery as its boundaries. There is a kind of promenade around the inner auditorium on the first floor. You get into the inner auditorium by walking under the galleries, which are nicely lighted—the lights create "stepping stones" on the floor. That is, you first come into a very low, softly lit space under the galleries; then you enter the inner auditorium where the space becomes high and cathedral-like.

Designer's model of the inner auditorium of the Albert Jorgensen Auditorium by Jerry Rojo with only a few seats set up

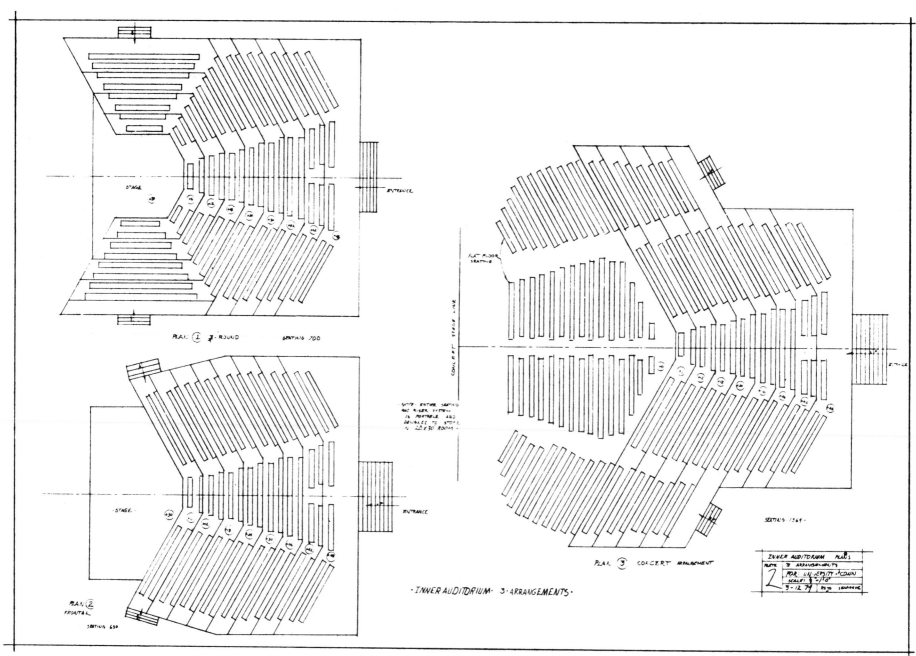

PLAN ① ¾ ROUND   SEATING 700

PLAN ② FRONTAL   SEATING 630

PLAN ③ CONCERT ARRANGEMENT   SEATING 1369

· INNER AUDITORIUM · 3 ·ARRANGEMENTS·

NOTE: ENTIRE SEATING AND RISER SYSTEM IS PORTABLE AND DESIGNED TO STORE IN 20' x 30' ROOM.

INNER AUDITORIUM PLANS
3 ARRANGEMENTS
FOR: UNIVERSITY · CONN
SCALE: ⅛"=1'-0"
3-12-74   ROJO SEABROOK

Ground plans of three seating arrangements of the inner auditorium by Jerry Rojo.

Incidentally, the original Auditorium stage was not used. And that became part of the problem—how to mask the immense stage opening. The solution was a series of wooden baffles similar to an acoustical shell. They created a cave-like effect, so that when they were lighted, anything beyond them—in this case the stage—was not seen by the audience. We put the stage for the inner auditorium in front of the old stage, simply drawing the curtain and masking it with the lighted baffles.

BMc: What was the original seating on the main floor of the Auditorium?

JR: About 2,700; the seating in the inner auditorium is 700.

BMc: How do you switch from 2,700 people to 700 people?

JR: The inner auditorium is comprised of approximately 2,000 platform units making up a riser system. Each unit is small enough and light enough to be handled by one man. Each unit is free standing on its own four legs; it locks into the next unit. The seats from the original Auditorium are portable; they are used in the inner auditorium. We simply designed the old seats into the inner auditorium space. Setting up a theatre that uses 2,000 platforms and 700 chairs is an immense job for any crew. Whenever they need to move the theatre, they hire university student help. It takes 12 people about one 8-hour day to make the transition. The units are stored in a room adjacent to the Auditorium. Each of the platforms making up the riser system is coded, of course. It is like a huge puzzle stored on wheeled carts. The carts are rolled into the storeroom, which is, I think, about 30' by 30' by perhaps 12' high. The whole theatre goes in there, rolled carpets and all, so that there is absolutely nothing left on the auditorium floor. Often there has been a 700-seat auditorium with a thrust stage in the space and then, two days later, the whole thing was gone.

BMc: Would this system be adaptable to a more conventional auditorium with a raked floor?

JR: I believe so. It would be a more complicated project, because you would need to develop legs to compensate for the rake.

BMc: Could a similar inner auditorium be set up in, say, a gymnasium?

JR: Yes, that would be a very logical place for this sort of project.

BMc: Could this modular idea also be used outdoors?

JR: Right.

BMc: You said that the stage of the inner auditorium is set up in front of the old stage. Is the new stage fixed? Or is it possible to change its shape?

JR: Over the years since 1971 that the theatre has been in use, Ed Seagrave, who handles all the productions, expanded the original idea. He has done things like removing the thrust stage of the inner auditorium to create a dance floor, with the orchestra on the main stage of the Auditorium and the spectators sitting at tables in a kind of horseshoe shape. When the regular theatre seats are removed there's the possibility for a cabaret.

BMc: There is room on each of those modular risers for tables and chairs?

JR: Yes. In a terrace-like situation. It works out very nicely for intimate events. In addition, he has now worked out a system of adding other units to the inner auditorium to accommodate different capacities. Besides the original 700-seat, three-quarter

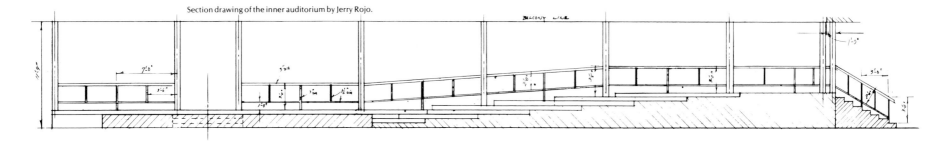

Section drawing of the inner auditorium by Jerry Rojo.

round system, Seagrave has devised two frontal seating arrangements—one which seats 1,200, the other seats about 500.

BMc: Does the inner auditorium use the lighting from the original space?

JR: Yes, in a way. In the ceiling there were "pot-lights," which were the original house lights. Ed has dropped in cables through those pot-lights and suspended light pipes from them. He does a miraculous job with that rigging, bringing in any kind of lighting.

BMc: Would it be possible to make a portable auditorium like this which also had self-contained lighting units?

JR: Yes. I think so. I would make light towers at the corners.

BMc: What problems are still to be solved in this theatre?

JR: Well, the problem of moving the inner auditorium persists. There is a lot of manpower cost to move 2,000 units and 700 chairs. It has been solved in part since Ed has worked out the schedule so that the theatre only has to set up two or three times a year.

BMc: One solution—it's an old circus showman's trick— is to have each seating unit on a flat-bed truck. Half of the unit drops down from the side of the truck to ground level; the other half remains in place on the truck bed. With a dozen units or so you can create a substantial "auditorium" that is totally mobile. You simply haul the trucks into place, flip down half the seats, and you're in business. When you want to dismantle the auditorium, you just reverse the process. The trucks move out to a warehouse and, of course, serve as storage racks for the seats. Something like those cargo containers used on ships could also be a way of handling this.

JR: You could just leave them out in the theatre parking lot in the rain or snow. It might be possible to incorporate your idea by having seating units inside the containers that could be slipped or rolled out into place, using the container trucks as the base.

Three Projects at The Space for Innovative Development

The Space for Innovative Development was a former church-school complex on West 36th Street in New York City, which was remodeled as a home for a number of new theatre and dance companies. Three projects were developed (but not built) for the Space by Jerry Rojo, in association with Brooks McNamara and Edmund Seagrave. The initial project was an attempt to create in the Alwin Nikolais-Murray Lewis dance studio, a former school gymnasium, a theatre which could be stored when the major portion of the floor space was required for dance classes and workshops. The audience seating unit, which is on wheels, may be broken down into three sections for storage around the studio's walls. The audience is seated on three levels and around three sides of an open space which is also used as a seating area, with the dancers performing in front of the audience unit.

Two additional projects centered around the chancel of the former church at the Space. There were separate concepts involved with the idea of turning the chancel into an open-space theatre. The initial scheme centered around metal galleries for audience seating to be suspended from the walls; the galleries were to be approached from a central complex of stairs and platforms located at one end of the room. A later concept substituted a kind of irregular "terrain" of plywood covered with carpet on the floor of the chancel for the galleries. The terrain was designed to accommodate both actors and spectators in a variety of relationships varying from full arena to three-quarter round.

⑥ The Nikolais-Lewis Room at the Space

BMc: The first of your projects was for Alwin Nikolais-Murray Lewis. When was it begun?

JR: 1971.

BMc: Has the project been constructed?

JR: No, the whole series of Space Projects is no longer being considered. The Space for Innovative Development converted a parochial church-school complex of the sort once common in New York City, with a gymnasium, a church, classrooms, bowling alleys, cloisters, and what not, all bound together in a single complex. The developers of the Space bought it, hired architects to go in and turn many of the rooms into open theatre spaces, fitted out with grids and lighting facilities. The Open Theater did projects there and the Nikolais-Lewis Dance Companies worked out of the Space. In 1974, it was made into a Third World performance center. In 1975, the building was abandoned.

BMc: You conceived the first of your space projects for Nikolais and Lewis?

JR: My negotiations were with Murray Lewis. The space he was using for his company was a former gymnasium. It had a flat floor, a small stage at one end (typical of old-fashioned schools), and a spectators' gallery at the opposite end, high off the floor and not accessible from the gymnasium proper. I think there had also once been an indoor track around the walls of the room.

BMc: What was the size of the space?

JR: About 70' long, 45' wide and 28' high. A nice room.

BMc: And what did Lewis want to do with it?

JR: It was a studio where large dance classes were conducted;

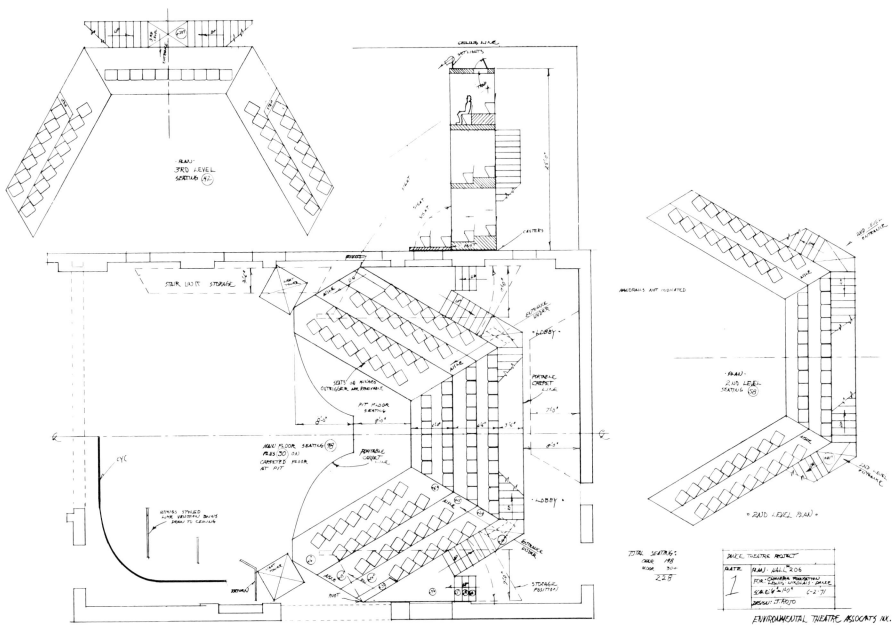

Ground plan and section drawing of The Nikolais-Lewis Room by Jerry Rojo.

some I saw involved 30 or 40 people. Dancers use up a lot of space. Lewis and Nikolais need a lot of space in order to have all those people in a workshop simultaneously. But they wanted to be able to have a theatre in that same room, or to devise some way that the floor could be cleared in the daytime for workshops and then late in the afternoon be converted to a theatre.

BMc: Was it possible to move the elements of the theatre out of the room for storage or did they have to stay there?

JR: I think there was a possibility of moving them out but it wasn't really very feasible because it would almost certainly have encroached on other areas. So, we finally decided that the theatre unit had to stay within that room.

BMc: Did you develop solutions that were discarded or rejected or modified?

JR: No. It was very informal. We kept talking over ideas and the final plan gradually evolved. I felt that the units should be stored flat against the walls during classes and workshops, but could be moved out from the walls to form a theatre for dance performances. We decided on a ground plan that would allow this and would take up minimal floor space in the stored position. The idea was very similar to galleries that you find in the French Quarter of New Orleans. I think that the concept might have come from there—since I went to Tulane and worked in New Orleans. The units developed as three movable, three-story galleries that could be joined together to form three sides of an octagon.

The audience enters much as they do at the Sarah Lawrence environment—from behind the audience seating. Then they begin to snake their way up through the galleries so that there is a certain built-in theatricality about the audience moving

through the space. I was intrigued by the complicated way the audience spreads out over these different levels.

BMc: The model shows that the audience comes in at the back, moves up some stairs to a low platform at one side, mounts another flight of stairs to another platform, then mounts still another flight of stairs to a higher platform. But they can move off any of these three levels. Can spectators see through the entire gallery unit to the stage?

JR: Yes. In this complex, the seats are fixed and, because it is a three-sided unit, they are raked so that they all face the center of the stage area. Dancers don't seem to like to work three-quarter round; most went to work in a frontal situation. That was one of the strictest requirements of the project, so that while there is an apparent thrust, the space between these three parts of the complex is really audience space, where people could sit on the floor, or possibly bring in chairs. The dance performance would actually take place in front of them.

BMc: So that the area between the three units is really rather like the orchestra floor in a conventional theatre rather than a thrust stage.

JR: Right. The units were to be constructed out of welded steel to create a lacy New Orleans wrought-iron feeling. And, of course, if it were made out of steel which is less bulky than wood, there would be less sight obstruction. The other thing is that since the structure is so massive, I felt that it needed to be built of something that was strong but fairly thin to keep it from overwhelming the room. A wooden structure would tend to dominate the space.

BMc: What were the technical problems concerned with the project—in terms of support, for example?

JR: We dealt with the problem only up to the point of submitting a design. We hadn't really gone very deeply into the question of load, but each of the units needed to bear a considerable load.

BMc: Are there possibilities for combinations other than the one shown in the model?

JR: No. The idea of the structure is that it interlocks, a three sided figure locked together with mitre joints which are very strong.

BMc: How about lighting?

JR: Well, a lighting scheme already existed. Nikolais-Lewis had installed a circuited pipe-grid system over the entire room.

BMc: Would it be possible to make the galleries a completely self-contained unit, to use them more or less as giant light towers?

JR: Yes, actually. In the project sketch, I show lights used on the top of the units. In the ceiling of the third story of each there was to be a trapdoor so that lights could easily be hung from the top. If a show were running every night, the lights would always be in focus when the units were in place. When the units were pulled apart to go to their storage positions, the lights would simply be unplugged.

BMc: In a modification of this, I suppose you could actually place the central booth in one of the units. In that case, you have a self-contained theatre which could be moved from place to place. In what other kinds of spaces might such a theatre be used?

JR: I think it might be a good solution for any high-ceilinged

Designer's model, front view, showing the seating levels. Designed by Jerry Rojo. Photo: Barry Rimler

space. The idea is that this theatre deals with audience vertically. It doesn't handle audience in an orthodox horizontal situation.

BMc: Could it be placed in other open spaces?

JR Yes, it would work nicely in a very large field house—with the area around it offering an interesting kind of "breathing space."

BMc: Here you've used a three-sided figure. Would it be possible to have as many as eight sides, all of which could lock together? In that case, one could choose to use three, four, five—up to eight sides. Would it also be possible to lock together in irregular combinations? Does such a thing interest you?

JR: Not really. That is very complicated and you end up spending a lot of time designing and adjusting machinery.

RS: When everything becomes mechanized, everything becomes compromised and you find, instead of gaining freedom and multi-purpose, you're locked up. Not only that, but the machinery starts to determine what you're doing. There's a fantasy about multi-purpose—that you can just keep adding flexibility. But you can't, because if you add it in one place, you take it away in another. The simpler a space, the less mechanical, the more flexible.

The thing to do is to use an environment as long as you want to, dispose of it, and make another. I think this represents a good carryover from orthodox scene design into environmental design. Orthodox scenography says: build a stage set for a play; when you're finished with the play, rip it down and build another stage set. The multi-purpose, architectural, mechanical approach says you only have to build one, it's very expensive, you use it for everything. I think they're both wrong. Orthodox designing is wrong because it uses only the stage—the house (which is most of the theatre) is fixed. I like to not be afraid of throwing away or cannabilizing the environment at the end of a production. There's nothing more flexible than starting from scratch. Every environment at the Garage starts from scratch and cannabilizes previous material and structures.

JR: I like to find out the problems of the group that's hiring me, find out what their theatre looks like, find out what the parameters are, and then design to solve their problems, rather than working on the principle of, "Can I do this, too?" I get very nervous about such things. Solve the problem and leave it that way.

BMc: Because both the Mobius Theatre and the Sarah Lawrence Project are wood construction, it should be possible to change your mind later and reorganize the space. Right?

JR: Right.

RS: The Nikolais-Lewis Project suggests something else to me. it seems that, in principle, there are two basic kinds of designs: the kind that anchors into the room—becomes part of the room—and the kind that is located in a room, like the Murray Lewis units, but may be attached or detached. When a design anchors into the room, when it transforms the room, then you have a new space. When it's something like the Space project which could be set up in a room, or in a stage house, or any place, then there is a temptation to make it more and more flexible. It's at that point with this kind of design—which, in a sense, is space within a space—that you have to draw the line and make it disposable, because if you make a space within a space complicated and super flexible it's going to end up as a white elephant. You're going to be stuck with it. So the Mobius might be ripped down at some point because it's wood and was built with student labor, but I still think it transforms the room in

which it was built and it would be a shame to rip it down.

BMc   There's a middle position that's important to mention. It is possible to build an environment that is sufficiently flexible so that you can change its character temporarily from one experiment to another. So, if I wanted to add some additional construction, some platforms, some ramps, and so forth, for the life of a particular production, I could do it.

RS: I wish we had had three or four spaces in addition to The Performing Garage so that somewhere the *Makbeth* environment could still be standing and somewhere else the *Commune* environment, because I'd like to continue to work in them both. But, at the same time they were beautiful to work in for a couple of years but I don't want to do every play in either one of them. Maybe my vanity hopes for New Performing Garages to sprout around the city where I could have left those things behind. But it's OK to rip them down. The worst thing is to build environments like *Commune* or *Makbeth* and do every production in them. Those spaces came out of particular problems connected with the plays. It's a sliding scale; I know that Nikolais and Lewis are involved with a certain style of dance that generates a special kind of space. Only if they change their style of dance will they need to change their space.

7 The Church at the Space: First Version

BMc: What room was designed for the second of the three Space Projects?

JR: A former church, built of stone and brick with high Gothic-arched windows, a vaulted ceiling, and colonnades running down two sides, producing a kind of cloister. There was once a balcony at one end which had been ripped down. The approximate dimensions are 100' by 40' with a ceiling about 60' high—a tall room. There were two plans for it. The first idea was to turn the space into a theatre that would be open and flexible enough so that any group—whether the Open Theater or the Nikolais Dance Company—could come in and work in its own way. One group might demand seating for only a hundred, a very intimate environment. Another might want 500 people sitting in a frontal situation. As I have found since, this is an impossible task because you end up constantly compromising one concept because of another. If you have an instinct about the kinds of things that are being done today, you can make a space serve each of them, but never all of them all the time. It is better to go for a limited number of possibilities.

BMc: How did you go about solving this particular problem?

JR;   The solution grew out of the architecture of the room. It is a very long, high room and I felt that the immediate solution was to get the audience off the floor. Those sheer, stone walls could become places for both the audience and the performers.

BMc: The idea, then, was to suspend much of the audience from the walls of this room. Describe what you wanted to do.

JR: The main entrance to the room is at the end where the altar had once been. The architects had cut a 12' high door there. I felt that it would be interesting to have a series of landings, stairways, and lobby areas leading from that door which would introduce you to the room and to the galleries which circle the room on three sides at approximately 20'.

BMc: The model suggests that you walked up a small flight of steps onto a platform. From there the audience seating areas, which are suspended from the walls, fan out around the room. You can see the entire room from the platform in somewhat the same way as the Murray Lewis units.

JR: Another interesting idea was that there was to be no fixed seating; there were simply tiered levels. These levels could be used as a performing area, and the audience could sit below on chairs or on the floor. As I suggested before, the main complex of stairs and platforms at the old altar end allowed spectators to get into the room but also could serve as a theatre itself. The cloisters that ran down the long axis of the room offered nice little niches for audience boxes, or for interesting little playing areas.

BMc: Then you could completely reverse the axis of the theatre: Instead of having the audience up, and the actors down, it was possible to put the audience down and the actors up on this complex of stairs, platforms, and galleries. I presume it would also be possible to create a kind of hybrid of those two approaches. What materials did you plan to use and why?

JR: The whole thing was to be done out of steel because I wanted to anchor the galleries into the walls, and keep the structure light. Because the room is narrow for its length I did not want to have posts supporting the galleries. They would present too much limitation of the space. So, I suspended the galleries from above, and I think that became the crucial issue when we considered materials. There was no problem with load, since as a church, it was designed to handle a tremendous audience.

BMc: How did you plan to use light?

JR: The galleries become very functional areas. I think if someone did a production on the floor in this space, the galleries would be beautiful places from which to run four or five spots, or projection equipment.

BMc: So you could use the front of the galleries as light pipes. I assume if you needed to place lights high you could fasten more pipes to the stanchions from which the galleries were suspended.

Ground plan and section-through of the first version by Jerry Rojo.

ENVIRONMENTAL THEATRE ASSOCIATES, INC.

8 The Church at the Space: Second Version

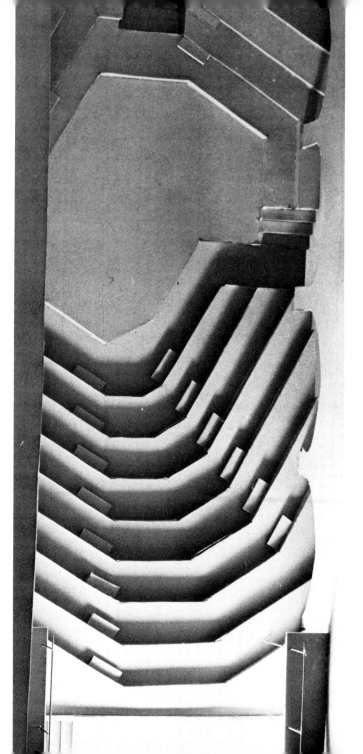

BMc: Did the third Space project present an evolution out of the one which we were just talking about?

JR: Probably not. A new executive director took over the space, and he had different ideas about what to do with the old church. So that rather than an evolution, I think the third project emerged as a totally different concept for the same room as in project 7.

BMc: I think the new director wanted essentially the same thing—a flexible space which could be used for a number of different kinds of performers and performances.

JR: Yes. Though perhaps he was more interested in a concept of audience seating than a concept related to the room itself. The new premise was that it was necessary to get "x" number of seats in the space. Our attempt was to get the maximum number of people into the room while trying not to deal with orthodox fixed seating, although that kind of seating could be set up if need be.

BMc: As I recall, we arranged the room so that people entered, as in the previous project, through the large door at the altar end. There they mounted some steps, and then walked down as one might at a football stadium, over the various levels, toward a stage area, which was near the center, a bit toward the opposite end. The axis was diagonal.

JR: I think the dynamics of a long rectangle like this room present a particularly difficult problem for a theatre; and one way to solve the problem is to set the theatre on a diagonal as we did here. It makes a much more interesting use of that room to break it with a diagonal axis. Everything is oblique; there's no 90-degree angle in the theatre. I think that helps to overcome the tension of that long rectangle by creating a counter tension.

Designer's model by Jerry Rojo. Bird's-eye
view of the second version. Photo: Barry Rimler

BMc: What materials did you plan to use in the construction?

JR: I had planned that the floor of the whole theatre would be carpeted, including the stage area. The carpeting would counterbalance and soften the stonework.

BMc: The effect of the thing becomes almost like a topographical map or a terrain with many levels.

RS: If you wanted a topographical effect there's the possibility in a room like this of more "hills" and "valleys." It could be more contoured without destroying sight-lines, and that would really give a rolling sense to the rectangle—creating gulleys and even perhaps, in the back, a deep valley where people could stand. I think one thing most people neglect when designing environmental theatre is the arrangement of the audience. Perhaps it's because in the proscenium theatre the audience arrangement doesn't really make much difference since spectators are in darkness. But in environmental theatre very often the lights spill over the audience even if you're not planning to light them or use them actively. The audience is part of the performance—not part of the drama, but part of the performance.

BMc: If there's a problem with this design, perhaps it was that we weren't opinionated enough. We began work with a series of negative ideas: you must have so many people in this room; you must not go above a certain height; you must make the space usable by a number of different kinds of groups.

Designer's model, looking from entrance
balcony across the theatre to the tech booth.
Model by Jerry Rojo. Photo: Barry Rimler

⑨ Leperque Space at the Brooklyn Academy of Music

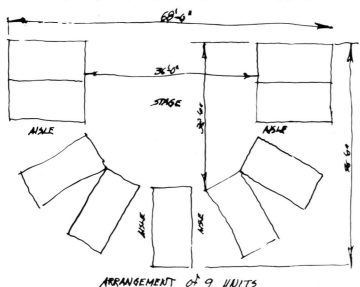

Portion of working drawing showing seating plan of the styrofoam units. Drawing by Jerry Rojo.

ARRANGEMENT of 9 UNITS

In 1973, Jerry Rojo, Brooks McNamara, and Edmond Seagrave developed for the BAM Leperque Space modular units that could be organized in a variety of ways as seating areas, stages, or a combination of audience and performing space. The project was not built. The modules were styrofoam bales encased in wooden frames covered with canvas "skin" locked together with a system of pipes dropped through holes in the bales. The bales were remarkably light but strong enough to bear great weights. They could be stacked to create an arena, a thrust stage, a frontal stage, and various environmental arrangements. The flexibility was achieved without heavy machinery.

JR: The open-space theatre is a very large hall, essentially it was a salon for parties and balls and that kind of thing, built around the turn of the century. It's a high room, fitted out with a technical booth, a grid-lighting system and velour draperies over the windows to control natural light in the room.

BMc: What was wanted for that space?

JR: A modular system of some kind that could easily be taken down and put together. Peter Brook was to be the first to use the system, but other groups were to use it as well. He was coming with "Ceremony of the Birds" within a month. So there was a rush. Brook wanted an open, flexible, simple space with seating for various numbers of people. His group was not only performing but doing public workshops, too.

BMc: What were the major considerations on the project?

JR: An essential was portability; whatever was done had to be set up and taken down, rearranged, and reorganized swiftly and easily by a fairly small crew. One of the major considerations was how to organize that large space within the room rather than trying to organize the whole room. Two to three hundred people had to be seated. We didn't know if we were going to create a terrain, terracing the people, or use some form of seating. The whole thing was fairly open-ended, but we were looking for something that would float within the space, acting as a kind of island in the room, rather than something that incorporated or encompassed the whole room.

BMc: Describe the solution.

JR: Well, we began to think of materials that could be easily handled and had some distinctive quality about them. We began to experiment with styrofoam. I found that by using a very high density styrofoam, which is a cellular material, it is possible to develop a relatively high construction strength. This was a material used in building construction.

BMc: It doesn't break down easily and it is possible to pile up a number of layers to create a platform, say, which is very light in weight but has considerable bulk.

JR: In our research on styrofoam we discovered that while it will withstand tremendous loads directly downward, wear and tear is high. It was necessary to encase the styrofoam somehow.

BMc: One possibility we thought of fairly early on was to make some kind of sleeve out of heavy-duty canvas. The result would be like a mattress, essentially, with the styrofoam inside a canvas bag; we called these bales.

JR: Basically, this would have been a heavy canvas bag, with a cover that could be zipped off, cleaned, and replaced. The bag would simply contain the styrofoam and would inhibit the breaking down of cells.

BMc: We also thought that the canvas-covered bags might have grommets on the edges, or loops of canvas, so that they could be lashed together in various patterns.

JR: Because of the lightness of styrofoam, heavy loads of actors or spectators would cause the bales to shift, so we needed some way to fasten the units one to another. But, in further developing the idea, we felt that the edges needed to be supported somehow. Rather than using the grommet and lashing scheme, I felt it would be more efficient to have the locking devices integral inside the unit, rather than outside. So we began by putting a wooden frame on the top and bottom of the bale. On the frame, we thought, would be fastened hinges or other kinds of hardware to help hold the bales together. The hardware would have been accessible through the canvas bag.

BMC: So essentially you were creating a kind of sandwich with a piece of light plywood, for example, on the top and bottom and the styrofoam in the center. How were top and bottom joined?

JR: The whole thing was encased in the heavy canvas. The idea was to create about 180 of these. The units were to be set up in one of two ways. One was a kind of children's building blocks arrangment. In another arrangement, bales could be put together in a very rigid audience-tiering effect. Peter Brook liked the simplicity of that line, and the squareness of it was like dominoes or cubes of sugar stacked up.

BMc: What was the size of the modules?

JR: They were 4' wide, 8' long, and 1' thick. The audience could sit on the bales, which were like big cushions.

BMc: How were you planning to tie them together?

JR: Through a system of rods that were dropped down through the holes bored in the bales. The dynamic here was that the mass held itself together, and the rods just kept it from shifting. It was like stacking up blocks; the rods just kept them in line. We felt that once the audience got on, the weight, coupled with the rods, would make an absolutely immobile unit. We designed a number of these units, figuring that the cost per unit would be about $100 at 1973 prices. We would make about 180 at first. The idea was ultimately to fill the room with them.

BMc: So there were many possibilities for organizing and reorganizing the space.

JR: Initially they wanted us to design wedge shapes, polygonal shapes and so on. But the idea of this design was not to create high-rises. We felt that rectangular bales would be best for developing a terrain with a Stonehenge quality. In any case, we could not go into high-rise for safety reasons.

BMc: It would be perfectly possible to use these elements to create a relatively low but complex terrain, one that possessed all kinds of peaks, hills, and valleys.

JR: Yes. Some panels could be locked together in larger modules. Projections could be thrown on them, perhaps. And they would also be strong enough to be suspended from cables so that people could walk on them.

BMc: They could also be hung on edge or braced in some way to create walls.

JR: And they could be easily stored; they are very light. Initially, I think, they were too light.

BMc: What did the weight finally turn out to be?

JR: We figured that the weight for each of them would be about 50 pounds.

Typical seating unit using styrofoam bales. Drawing by Jerry Rojo.

BMc: So it was perfectly possible for a single person to shift it.

JR: Yes. But the project was not built. We couldn't find a firm that would bid on it because of the very short time in which it had to be done. There were also a lot of skeptics who resisted it.

RS: A lot of what keeps new work from getting done is stupid resistance—I'm using the word "stupid" to mean slow-witted—and conservatism, not only about people's reputations, but about safety codes that were developed for other purposes in other times.

BMc: There's something else, too, that is a holdover from the traditional scene-designer's concept of what one can do and what one cannot do on stage. The typical designer works out of a series of self-imposed limitations. He thinks first of what he can't do, and then works from that. He's been taught to build his concepts around a relationship to the stage, and technical equipment that has only so many possibilties in relationship to lights and stage, and so on. Consequently, what he perfects in his career is a series of brackets that reduce the possibilities for him rather than expanding them.

RS: What's necessary, of course, is a laboratory. One of the advantages of having your own theatre is that you can experiment. It has been years since a designer or an environmentalist has been the originator of a project. Today we expect that directors or producers are originators of projects. But why not scenographers? In the late 19th century we had two scenographers who were originators, and they had terrific impact—Appia and Craig. But after them, the directors took over, and it's still the directors and the producers who remain the originators. The playwrights have been said to hold power, but they don't have any actual power in the theatre.

BMc: There have been some periods in the past when the scenographer really determined much of what was going on. The classic battle between Jonson and Inigo Jones is an interesting case in point. The masques proceeded out of Jones' vision of what scenography could do. In many ways, his designs were the heart of the productions. Other cases in point are the Victorian melodramas with their "sensation" scenes based on very complex scenic effects. These effects often were the central impulse behind the writing and production of the plays. Interestingly enough, because of our strange mentality about theatre, those periods dominated by scenic effect are considered infertile. But they're not infertile at all, quite the contrary. They simply place their emphasis on scenography rather than on the literary aspects of productions.

RS: Right. Scenographers ought to originate productions today, just as they have done in the past. It's been assumed—and I challenge that assumption—that the environmentalist waits until he's invited, finds out what the limitations are, designs something, gets it approved, and then builds it. If the approval doesn't come, it's stopped. The argument about who controls the play—the writer, the director, the scenographer, the actor—is ridiculous. It should depend on the project. Jerry ought to have the opportunity to originate a project—to originate it without making himself a director any more than I make myself an actor. The problem to be worked out might be fundamentally spatial, and plugged into that problem are problems of directing acting, and thematics or playwrighting. I think it's very important that we come to the point where the true collaborative nature of production is that the center of the project can be either acting, directing, scenography, or writing. Or maybe something unthought of yet.

BMc: So you see the possibility of contemporary productions that throw their weight to the scenographic aspect of theatre?

RS: The scenographer can be the ultimate authority, just as in a director's theatre, the director is; or in an actor's theatre, the actor is; or in the commercial theatre, the producer is; or in the writer's theatre, the writer is. It's simply giving the scenographer his or her due. I would like to invite Jerry, not only to work with me as we've done before, but to come and do a project where he functions as the chief person—not necessarily as the director; he might have a director working for him, just as a director has a scenographer working for him.

JR: But I think all of this happens in good design. I've always felt that my richest rewards as a designer have come from directors who are open to new concepts, and those concepts really fix the production.

BMc: This is a relatively rare thing in our time. Usually the design is an adjunct to the apparent center of the work.

JR: I agree. The design usually comes after somebody already has a project. A designer is hired to "realize" it.

RS: But one falls into certain habits, and I think it would be good for scenographers to start out with their own ideas, whatever they may be, and to see them through. A spatial idea can precede the selection of the play. There always have to be compromises—obviously a director makes compromises with everybody but frankly the compromises are often manipulations to achieve certain actions. I'm suggesting that it would be enriching for the scenographer to have his own way.

BMc: That means that a production could become a laboratory for exploring scenography rather than—as it characteristically is—a laboratory for research in acting and directing.

RS: Meyerhold did it. Meyerhold was both a director and a scenographer in that sense. A true theatre laboratory should give each aspect of the theatre a chance to have its sway over all others, as an alternative to a completely collaborative situation. It would be interesting to see what would happen if Jerry were to present spatial ideas not subject to anybody's veto.

JR: That's a unique situation.

RS: It's not unique for actors, directors, or writers.

BMc: Typically it is the designer's work that gets homogenized. Something that interests me as a scenographer is the idea of an "actorless theatre," one in which effects become a whole theatrical performance.

RS: Happenings did that, and some movies. Let's put it another way. There has always been a mystique about the "artist" in the theatre so that the artist controlled the whole production. Because designers and environmentalists have been identified with technical people, their work isn't felt to be as artistic as the work of actors or directors. On the other hand, Jerry and I work collaboratively. Jerry could have veto power. It would be fun for me as a director; it would put me in a situation that I haven't experienced.

BMc: It would give you fits!

RS: Really? One thing that's held back scenographic innovation, although it's supposedly advanced it, is the idea that it's enough to conceive of something great without following through into the actual construction. The kind of approach where the scenographer give his best ideas without building them is a cop-out. One expects actualization from a director, an actor, or a playwright. Artaud alone was able to get away with

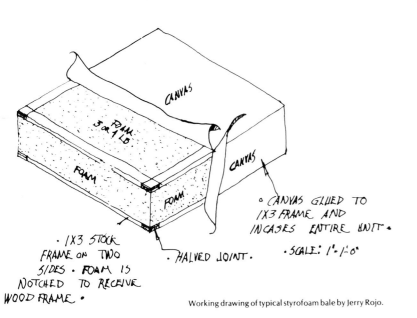

CANVAS

FOAM 3 or 1 LB

FOAM

FOAM

CANVAS

° CANVAS GLUED TO
1X3 FRAME AND
INCASES ENTIRE UNIT.

° SCALE: 1"=1'-0"

· 1X3 STOCK
FRAME ON TWO
SIDES · FOAM IS
NOTCHED TO RECEIVE
WOOD FRAME ·

· HALVED JOINT ·

Working drawing of typical styrofoam bale by Jerry Rojo.

mere visions. I think one of the contributions that Jerry is making is that these projects are either built or buildable. If they weren't built, it's not because they are "ideal concepts." They're designed for actual spaces, spaces that exist. I think that the "ideal concepts" approach (Keisler, Craig, and so on) represents an academic tradition. In theatre, ideas that can't be realized have no value. They have no historical weight. They debilitate rather than energize.

BMc: Those ideas have percolated down in a completely academic way, changing much of the exterior shape of scenography without changing the basic 19th-century principles of orthodox design. The principles are always there underneath: We continue to get the same old romantic, proscenium, "technical" stage, with an overlay of the ideas of the great innovators.

JR: You know, for a while I felt guilty that in my portfolio there are no studies of *Macbeth, Hamlet,* and whatnot. I have a tremendous resistance toward doing model studies. I think in terms of specific projects. Even when Richard said, "Let's do some studies of *Commune.*" I would go away and do something, but it never came out in substantive form. Because I know from working with Richard that there's a time when we get down to brass tacks, and that's the time when decisions are made in very specific ways. Up to that point, everything remains academic. You must start with the real problem, and when you've got the problem, you can find the solution.

BMc: Related to this, Richard once defined a contrast between what he called a "theatre arts" approach where everybody—the director, designer, actor and so on—goes off in a different direction and creates something, with the result a kind of homogenization of all of their relatively unrelated efforts. He contrasted this with an "art of the theatre" approach, in which everything grows out of a solution to the problem. It is a really organic approach, in which design is clearly bound into the total work.

RS: Right. And I think that the second approach depends upon a certain kind of materialism—there's no more material art than the theatre, and I think materialism is good for it. It is the idea of planning a production not in space, but in *this* space; not in terms of acting, but with *these* actors; not in terms of playwrighting, but with *this* play. That's why I have to have the Garage, or something like it. I'm not the kind of director who can say, "I've got a play, now let's find a space," I really have to root in a space. When we did *Victims of Duty* in New Orleans, for example, I had to be in the studio theatre, Le Petit Théâtre du Vieux Carré, before I could think of the design. And now that the Garage is there, everything is worked out in its terms. Just as the Greeks had a certain number of actors, and a certain stage on which they could work, or the Elizabethans had their characteristic theatre space, I need the limitation that forces creativity.

BMc: We keep coming back to the same point; the idea of a fundamentally opinioned approach, rather than an eclectic one which attempts to accommodate everybody or account for all things. The approach we are defining here seems only to account for the things one chooses to account for and forgets about the rest.

JR: There's another tradition here, too. Take the classics, for example: there's a settled way of doing those plays. Once everybody agrees on the way classic plays are to be done, you can do designs for them, if you subscribe to that kind of theatre, but I think that's a non-premise for theatre.

BMc: In fact, it's only an historical problem that is restated for each production, rather than allowing each production to present its own problem.

RS: The business of limitations is interesting because it defines the difference between company and cast. If you have a company, and a space, and people you're going to work with, you have certain givens, and you work. You are, in a sense, locked together, and something happens. If you have a cast rather than a company (as both the commerical and most regional theatre do) then you say, "Well, I can find this person to play this role, and that person to play that role." I don't find that kind of casting creative. It encourages laziness. Having too much, you never face the situation that confronts a football team where there are 11 people on the field at a given time, and you have to play the game with 11—you can't decide that it would be nice to play with 12. In fact with the "special team" strategy, football loses its interest. If you have open auditions, and hire for each show, all of a sudden you're not really rubbing up against the problem. You're going around it.

JR: It's an interesting notion about intentionally setting limitations.

RS: That's the way it is in rituals and sports. They provide the best spectacles, and they're the best because there's a tension between limitations and the event happening within these limits. After several months of the run of *Commune*, five people left the company in April, 1971. Instead of replacing all of them we condensed the piece—restructured it for six persons. It was a much more coherent production when it reopened in July. Each production in the Garage must come to terms with the limitations of the space. The ropes and pulleys system of *Mother Courage* is possibly the best solution to the problems of that play in that space. A wagon would not work. Necessity is the mother of theatrical invention, and the largest part of necessity is that you're locked into limitations. Changes are wrought within the limitations. It's good ecology.

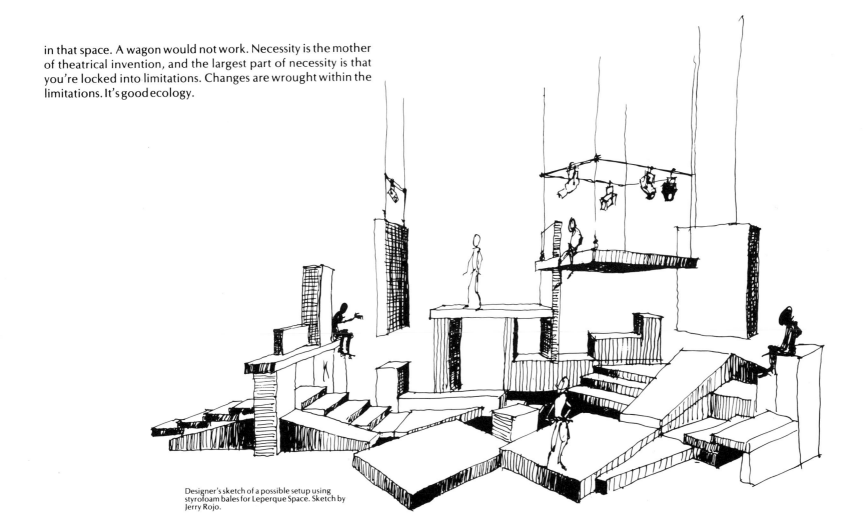

Designer's sketch of a possible setup using styrofoam bales for Leperque Space. Sketch by Jerry Rojo.

The Same Space: Different Environments

10 Dionysus in 69

The Performance Group, co-directed by Richard Schechner, was founded by him in New York in 1967. A year later the Group acquired the Performing Garage, a former factory in the Soho area south of Greenwich Village. There the Performance Group has presented nine productions, *Dionysus in 69, Makbeth, Commune, Concert, The Tooth of Crime, The Beard,* and *Mother Courage and Her Children, A Wing and a Prayer* and *Sekonnet Point.* Each year from one to three new works are done. The Performance Group is an example of a theatre company which uses the same space, constructing a different environment for each new production.

The first of the Performance Group's environments was *Dionysus in 69* designed by Jerry Rojo. Basically the environment consisted of two 19'-high wooden towers dividing the space diagonally into thirds. A three-story gallery stood along the north wall and three low platforms were used at various points around the room. The audience could sit or stand in any part of the environment and, although much of the performance took place in the center of the room, all of the space and all of the levels were used by the peformers as well as the spectators.

RS: *Dionysus in 69* was begun in January, 1968. But it was not until March 1st that we took possession of the Garage.

BMc: What was the Garage like at the beginning?

RS: I think I saw it a couple of months before Jerry did. In the beginning there was a large space heater in the center of the room hanging down about 12' into the room on a long elbow which angled out from the southwest wall into the center of the space.

BMc: What is the size of the space?

JR: 50' by 35' by approximately 20' high.

RS: The building was constructed around 1960 as a metal stamping factory between two already existing old buildings. They threw up four steel girders, two on each side, and two cross girders and constructed the building on that frame. The ground floor has a pit that was used for the guts of the stamping machine. The space was never actually a garage, but we called it The Garage because the first time I saw it there was a garbage truck parked in it. Since we decided to call ourselves The Performance Group, it seemed appropriate to call it The Performing Garage. The floor is concrete and the walls are cinder block, and there is a 12' high, overhead door opening onto Wooster Street (the east side of the building) and two small windows where we later put two air conditioners.

BMc: It's possible to enter through the garage door, although that has never been used as an entrance, or through each of two small doors on either side of it.

RS: Yes. One of those entrances opens onto Wooster Street; the other opens into a hallway from which you go out to Wooster Street.

There is another very important space, about 10' wide by 24' deep, and as high as the main space, opening into the main room off the northwest corner. We use it as storage and as "backstage" and as a tech area.

JR: The pit is about 40' long by 8' wide and 7' deep. Although the floor of the Garage is concrete, for the third production, *Commune,* we built a 3/4" plywood floor on a 2' by 3' framing member, so there's an all-wooden floor in the theatre now. The pit is also trapped over with plywood.

BMc: What about the second floor?

RS: We did not possess the entire building until September,

1968, so *Dionysus* opened without us having any rights to the upstairs. It was a living loft with exactly the same floor space as the Garage, although the ceiling is only 10' high. The southeast corner is occupied by a kitchen and, off that, a bathroom. There is also a small space heater, on the south side, and on the east wall there are five windows that open onto Wooster Street. At the back, there is a small room just like the one downstairs, but with a lower ceiling.

For the run of *Dionysus* we used that back room as an office, and the rest as a lobby and workshop area. Then, with *Makbeth*, we converted the upstairs into the *Makbeth* maze, which we will talk about later, a dressing room area, and a lobby. During *Commune*, we ripped down the maze and built a small office in the southeast corner. The main room became a lobby and the room in the back became living quarters for a couple of members of the Group. We also lowered the ceiling so that we had a storage area above the back room; then, as *Commune* went on, we built two more living spaces upstairs.
The whole upstairs became balkanized, and could not be used for workshops or anything else. In the fall of 1973, we converted the upstairs into a second performance and workshop space with room for about 75 spectators. We did *The Beard* and *A Wing and a Prayer* there. Over the tech area is a room which is now used as office, green room, and storage area. Actually we used the roof in the spring of 1975 to stage a short play.

BMc: Will you say a word or two about the character of the Garage as a building and about the quality of the larger environment around it—the Soho area?

RS: The Garage, for my taste at least, is almost perfect in its proportions. The acoustics are impeccable: You can speak in a low conversational tone and be heard all over; the

The Performing Garage. *Dionysus in 69*; the audience waiting to enter.
Photo: Fred Eberstadt

reverberations are neither so slight as to make dead sound nor so lively as to make echoes. The space itself is flexible because it is not pretty. You don't go in there and say, "Oh, my god, if I make any changes I'll be ruining some kind of architectural landmark." The Garage has a kind of let's live in it feeling, the feeling that work can be done there. We have ripped it up and taken it apart inside and put in environments, and taken them down again. Also, there is a trapdoor in the ceiling of the downstairs space. So you can get between the two spaces without going outside or up stairways. Overall the quality of the space is beautifully flexible and workable.

We've put in heating and air-conditioning. We brought in two electrical lines, one in 1968 and one in 1972, so that we have more than enough power (though no money to pay for it). We've got two sets of dimmers downstairs, and we've run cable upstairs where we can plug in another control board.

JR: I'd like to add a couple of points about the Garage's architecture. I think it's important that the walls are almost totally without pipes and the other kinds of plumbing that are often found in such a room. I think that is very fortunate. I like a room that has structural irregularities, nooks and crannies, and this room has a certain amount of that, but the fact that the walls are clear is important because it simplifies building. Clear, sound walls become important when you're looking for anchor points. The fact that the walls at the Garage are of cinder block means that you can suspend tremendous loads from them; you don't always have to come up from the floor with structures, you can use the walls to support a lot of the weight.

BMc: You might say a word about the quality of the Soho neighborhood as an architectural environment.

RS: The quality of the neighborhood has changed con-siderably since we moved there; we were one of the first theatre groups in the area. In 1968 there were a number of artists who were using working lofts in Soho, but there were few galleries, restaurants, or theatres—very little street life. Since we've moved in, Soho has become the liveliest artistic neighborhood in New York. It has a double quality: during weekdays, much of the neighborhood is light industry, trash collection, rag warehouses. Most of the buildings are five to seven stories; they're industrial buildings but a lot of them have been converted into artists' residence lofts, some of them quite splendid. Architecturally, the neighborhood ranges from the Garage, which is one of the newer buildings, back into the 19th century.

BMc: Yes, back almost to the middle of the 19th century; it's the greatest collection of cast iron-front buildings in the world.

RS: It has been declared an historic landmark area, and I think as the years go by, it'll only get more and more beautiful as those buildings get restored. But, the character will change as the workers move out and the rich move in. Already, on Prince Street, co-op lofts go for $75,000 or more. At night and on weekends, the feel is of an outdoors community with lofts and gallery-looking.

JR: Although it has always been an industrial area, artists moved in illegally. Because of the large number of artists who lived in the area, the City was recently forced to recognize it as residential.

BMc: There's been a lot of money spent on Soho in the last few years and in the view of a number of the artists who live there, all that money has not changed its character for the better. There are those who resent very much some of the fast money and new galleries, the sense of exploitation that pervades the place. Not

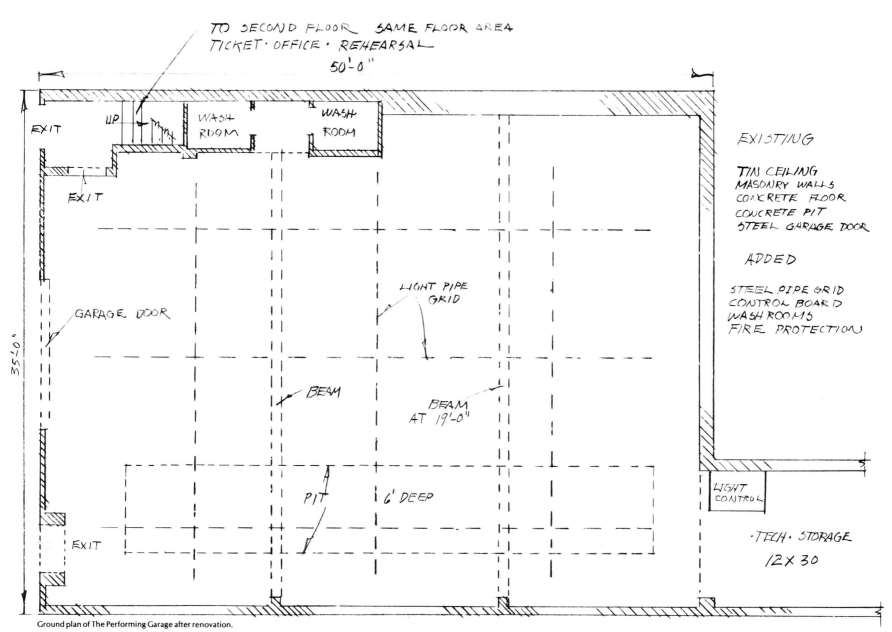

TO SECOND FLOOR SAME FLOOR AREA
TICKET·OFFICE·REHEARSAL
50'-0"

EXIT

UP

WASH
ROOM

WASH
ROOM

EXIT

EXISTIUG

TIN CEILING
MASONRY WALLS
CONCRETE FLOOR
CONCRETE PIT
STEEL GARAGE DOOR

ADDED

STEEL PIPE GRID
CONTROL BOARD
WASH ROOMS
FIRE PROTECTION

35'-0"

GARAGE DOOR

LIGHT PIPE
GRID

BEAM

BEAM
AT 19'-0"

PIT   6' DEEP

LIGHT
CONTROL

EXIT

·TECH·STORAGE

12 X 30

Ground plan of The Performing Garage after renovation.

PERFORMING GARAGE AFTER RENOVATION

long ago there were stickers plastered all over the area, which said, "Soho sucks, bring back the trucks"!

RS: Well, there is a lot of fast money, but I like the atmosphere.

BMc: What did you want to do with The Garage for *Dionysus in 69*?

RS: I think it's important to know that, because of the way I work, my initial idea is never the one that I finish with. My first goal was to get the Garage warm enough to do workshops in it. The second idea, which we carried into the production, was to make it plush. That came from the production of *Victims of Duty* I had done in New Orleans with Frank Adams, Paul Epstein, and Jerry Rojo. For *Victims* we did a whole room with rugs.

BMc: What do you mean by "plush"?

RS: I mean a room in which performers, working with very few clothes, feel warm and could keep from getting hurt on the cement floor. I wanted a room in which audiences would feel they were in a womb. The room has to be sensuous, to have the tone of a Persian pleasure palace, because *Dionysus* has that kind of feeling. It also had to have in it the red of blood, and the warmth of blood—I wrote an essay about *The Bacchae* called "In Warm Blood." So we went out and found dozens and dozens of rugs. I also felt—and I think Jerry and I agreed and fed each other—that vertical space had to be used. Somehow we had to get both audience and performers off the ground. I don't like stage settings where the performers go up and the audience doesn't, like Peter Brooks *Midsummer Night's Dream*. Unless the audience can walk on the balcony or swing on the swings, too, the concept is only half-achieved: all it does is separate the audience from the performer with the result that the performer is constantly saying. "See, I can do something that you can't do."

So, in *Dionysus* I wanted the audience and performers to share the same space, the same dangers, the same environment. But the exact form of that environment only took shape during April or May, only a few weeks before the performance opened. The initial impulse was height, warmth, sensuality, and flow.

BMc: Did you come to any early solutions that you discarded?

RS: The *Dionysus* book talks about a lot of the improvisations that went on, and they were important. We explored the space of the room, and we explored madness and ecstasy and what it meant to run around that neighborhood. We did one improvisation which took the performers to the roofs of Soho. The women were "set free," and the men had to go out and chase them down, and bring them back to the Garage. The result was that the police came because there were reports of people running across the roofs in the neighborhood. When the women were all captured and brought in, Pentheus had them put into the pit, where they were like animals and sex objects, because that's part of his fantasy. And they rebelled and killed him. There was also an improvisation involved with scrubbing the floor. The pit was filled with hot water, and we scrubbed it and invented work chants as we cleaned the room.

The Group did a lot of the actual building work on *Dionysus*—more than at other times because we didn't have any technical people and we had to do the construction ourselves. We decided to paint the room white—I think that decision was made before we brought Jerry in—because I despise theatre black, I despise the idea of not having light bounce, I despise the idea of trying to make the room into something that it isn't. So, as a reaction against that, I said, "What's the opposite of black? White! That will kill all this idea of fancy lighting. That will kill the idea that the lights should all come from one direction." We built scaffolds to paint from and the idea of scaffolds became integrated into the exercises. When Pentheus took over, for example, he climbed a scaffold and sent everybody down to the floor; when the people rebelled, they shook the scaffold and came up after him. So that the idea of using scaffoldlike structures was built in very early. Then I called Michael Kirby, who at that time was then known as the guy who did Happenings, as the author of a book on Happenings and as the editor of the Happenings issue of TDR. He was not into theatre very much, he was a sculptor, but he was a close friend of mine, and so I said, "Why not design an environment?" We talked about ideas like a forest of trees or hills, which would be abstract, but which were essentially constructivist. Somehow they didn't work. Jerry got involved at that point, I don't recall exactly how, but it was out of our first meeting that we got the idea of the two towers, which were the dominant structures of the environment. Basically, they were a transformation of the scaffold idea, and the platforms added later were an elaboration of that same idea. There's one other thing that I'd like to return to—the 3′ by 12′ black mats that you see in all the pictures of *Dionysus*, which we still use for some of our exercises. When we had only a cement floor we bought black rubber mats to work on. They were the only thing we could stand on, or keep warm on, or do headstands or other exercises on, so throughout the workshops the black mats came to be home. In May, very late, we bought rugs because we found a carpet store where they told us that for $150 we could take all the used rugs we wanted. They covered much of the room and some of the walls. The black mats were then placed in the center area, which became the "holy" area, the special place. The mats became an anchor on the ground.

BMc: Jerry, how did you get involved?

JR: I was teaching at the University of Connecticut, when in

1966, I went back to Tulane University, where I got my Master's, to work on a PhD. But specifically I went there with the idea of working with Richard. I knew of him through TDR. I had been brought up in the scene-painting tradition. I had done a lot of box sets. I wasn't unhappy. In New Orleans, I took Richard's classes and got to know him by working on his production of *Victims of Duty*. When I went back to Connecticut Mike Gregoric and I got the idea of having Richard come up and review an intermedia production of ours, *The Runoff*. Richard saw *The Runoff*, and later that spring he called me and asked me if I would help him on *Dionysus*. The first thing he showed me were some back-of-the-envelope sketches. The sketches had a loose resemblance to towerlike structures.

BMc: Can you describe what you did to the Garage?

JR: Initially we designed two towers 8′ long by 4′ wide and 19′ tall with five levels in each.

BMc: How were these towers placed in the room?

JR: Diagonally opposite to each other, one in the northwest corner, the other in the southeast corner, facing into the center area. The towers were primarily for the audience, but we were aware that the performers would also use them.

BMc: What were the towers made of?

JR: Each of the main posts of the towers was made of 6″ by 6″ construction fir. When we ran out of money, we began to take three, 2′ by 6″ planks and bolt them together for posts.

BMc: What did you do to these towers in the way of finishing, and why?

JR: I was interested in getting a kind of Oriental look. Actually I wasted space to get that look. For example, I used a lap joint that was a little more decorative than what I'm using now and there was an overall loss of about 12″ in height because of it. There was a certain amount of calculated decorativeness built into those towers. But they weren't painted, or stained.

RS: That decorativeness is news to me. Up to this moment I thought they were all they had to be—purely functional.

BMc: You say they were more decorative than they would be now. Can you expand on that?

JR: It's hard to describe. I used 4″ by 6″ vertical posts, and the framing members were 2′ by 6″, which didn't need to be there for purely functional purposes. But aesthetically, I felt they were needed to achieve a special look.

BMc: In your work on later environments you have largely abandoned the idea of anything other than pure function.

JR: Yes, mainly because I've come to agonize over that 6 inches, or 8 inches or 12 inches of space that is wasted on decoration. It's not really wasted, I suppose, because I think you always come down to using it somehow, but I'm constantly looking for that extra few inches for another set of stairs, a riser, or a little extra height. I find that I abandon any so-called aesthetic notions now, in order really to solve the spatial problems. If anything "aesthetic" in the traditional sense comes out of my work, it's because there's a certain rhythm within the space, but not because of framing techniques, or calculated artistic relationships.

BMc: Aside from the two towers and the black mats in the white room, what else was used when *Dionysus* first opened?

JR: Let me give some background to that. I think that Richard and I have created more elaborate environments over the years as we became more affluent. But we've always worked from a structure which he could accept, and on which later changes were made. He always accepts or rejects a concept; he doesn't toy with it. From there, he injects into it certain things that he feels he wants personally, and that I feel he's entitled to have and ought to have. I always attempt to provide them. Then there's another phase, after that, where he adds new elements as the production needs them.

BMc: Can you give me an example?

JR: In *Dionysus*, the rugs came that way and so did new units on the north wall. Also there were other subsidiary tower units added; as I recall, there were two of them, one in a corner, and one at an entrance.

RS: What happens here is that theory comes after practice. The theory is that the people who use the space print themselves on it, put themselves in it. In orthodox stage design, the concept is quite different—the idea is like that of an envelope, really. There's an envelope and there's a message in it: the envelope should be well-designed, but it has nothing whatever to do with what your letter says. I believe that this a false approach, destructive, and fundamentally inartistic. The space ought to be part of those who use it.

Jerry and I work by taking off from the performer. If Jerry were there every night he would continue to add to it, but at a certain point, because of the necessity to go on and do other work or whatever, he's not there anymore. He doesn't come in until a good deal of rehearsing and exploring has been done and then at a certain point he withdraws. But I am there most of the time and the performers are there all of the time, and I think it's very important for the space to become personalized by all of us.

Let's take specific examples: In *Dionysus* some of the smaller

The Performance Group warms up before a performance of *Dionysus in 69*. Photo: Fred Eberstadt

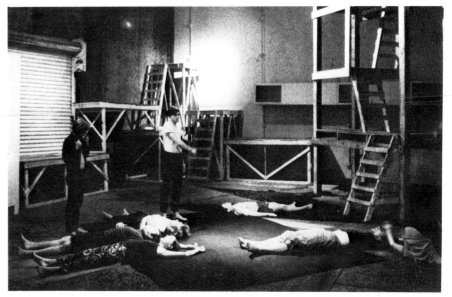

towers were movable. They were moved around quite a bit, sometimes because I wanted them moved around, sometimes because the performers wanted them moved. The staining of the walls and platforms with blood, which became an important element in the environment of *Dionysus*, was obviously done by the performers' own hands during actual performances. I never told them, "Put blood here, and don't put it there." It appeared wherever they happened to put it while they were working in the play; the placement was unconscious perhaps, but no one can deny that those blood stains in the space were an important part of the design.

In *Commune* I think this became even more important, because the performers each took over space within the larger space, which he or she made into his or her own house. The performer could bring whatever he or she wanted into this house. Some brought in pillows or cushions; some put pictures up; some put temple bells or other decorations; each could light it any way he wanted. So in *Commune*, there were particular places: Clementine's house, Susan Belinda's house, Lara's house, Bruce's house, David Angel's house, and these places became very personal; if we went in and took out certain little details, they got very upset. These houses were like mini-sets within the set. If you went into a house you would see that it had, say, a picture of Jim Griffiths' family, which he put into Fearless' house. Furthermore, in the *Commune* environment, we gave the audience chalk of different colors when they came in, and over a period of more than a year, they drew on the walls, on the ceiling, and on the structures themselves.

BMc: So that the design was constantly being transformed as towers were moved from place to place in *Dionysus* and graffiti chalked and rechalked in *Commune*.

RS: Right; Let me add two more details of *Dionysus* which I think are very important. On one side of the Garage, there was an overhead door leading to a perfectly blank wall. It didn't go anywhere. Bill Finley, without me knowing it, went out and got a 4' by 6' blowup of himself with a flower in his mouth, and one night at the end of the play—he was playing Dionysus—he pulled that door up, and there was his picture. It was really a big moment in the play; it's there in the movie that Brian de Palma, Bruce Rubin, and Bob Fiore made of *Dionysus*.

Another example is from Sam Shepard's *The Tooth of Crime*. Becky and Hoss (Joan MacIntosh and Spalding Gray) share an area near the bed. I told them: "You live here, this is your house, decorate it; you're stars, put up your pictures." They went to Fred Eberstadt, one of our photographers, and they had pictures taken in minks and with different trophies. And they gathered other things—mirrors, posters—and put them all together, and they found a scale for their space. Other performers helped too, especially Liz LeCompte who has an excellent visual sense. So, what it all amounts to is that the director determines a frame inside which things can happen—a conceptual frame. The environmentalist builds a structure, and the performers live in that structure. Those who are there every day live in it, just as you live in your own house.

BMc: In traditional theatre "good taste," "consistency," and so on, are the canons of design. What's the function of good taste and consistency here?

RS: A company like The Performance Group, by the very nature of our relationships, creates a kind of family. Consistency, therefore, is the web of relationships among us. If we are at each other's throats, as we were while preparing *Makbeth*, there's no reason to pretend otherwise. *Makbeth* was sparse and bitter because we were sparse and bitter. The environment spatializes

The performers march into Wooster Street at the end of *Dionysus in 69*. Photo: Fred Eberstadt

what is going on among the company—these goings on are also the life of the play, the life of the characters. As far as "good taste" and all that other garbage is concerned, well, it's all created to defend parochial "professional" rights. A kind of actual life must be lived in the theatre. Actual life is not reached by going home and studying a role. Actual life is lived here and now in the ongoing workshop, rehearsal, or performance experience.

BMc: You're suggesting that there is a certain kind of coherence that stems from the event itself and from performers working with each other, and that these organizing principles are not really involved with good taste.

RS: The principles are concentric rather than sequential. In orthodox theatre the writer sets up a frame, and everything done thereafter must be done within that frame. Then the director sets up a frame, smaller than the writer's because it is based on the writer's, and everything must also be done within that frame. The designer sets up another frame which fits within the director's and then the actor does the same, so that each of the frames are reductions of previous frames. Environmental theatre superimposes frames on each other, and all the frames are flexible, so that if, at the last moment, the performer finds something that ought to change the concept of the director, the designer, the author—then changes can happen because the frames are not sequential but concentric with the largest frame being the loosest. The audience makes the largest frame, and changes in audience effect all other frames.

BMc: You're saying that the question of good taste or good design is irrelevant because, in the process of rehearsal and performance, the environment is never the same. There's only the evaluation of the group, bringing to the environment whatever coherence it produces.

JR: It seems to me that when a group is living in a space, that space becomes very precious. To put something unnecessary in there, something illusory, denies the fundamental idea of the space. It's analagous to a highway. When I look at an aerial view of some maze of highways in California, I say to myself, how else could you get around? If automobiles are going to be your way of moving, then those highways are beautifully designed. They do what they are supposed to do—and no more. There are few errors in good highway constuction. Our highways are the most beautifully designed in the world.

BMc: You said to me once that you view the problems of the environment more as an engineer than as a designer. If that's so, your principles are those of good engineering, rather than of "good design" in the traditional sense.

JR: All good designs have a sense of rhythm and a sense of unity. Perhaps rhythm and unity are being redefined now. When you look at the highways I just mentioned, you find that signs are repeated at certain intervals—and that's rhythm. There is a flowing of whiteness and blackness and, as you drive, you see the repetition of white lines—those are rhythms.

RS: It depends where you think the sources of creativity lie, I suppose. In orthodox scene painting, as I understand it, everything is supposed to be conscious, worked out in detail from rendering to conception. But I think there's another aesthetic: the aesthetic of preparation rather than rehearsal. This is true of Australian Aborigines practicing for initiation, Balinese getting ready for a trance dance, or Jerry Rojo and The Performance Group building a space—it is not the abandonment of discipline, it's an understanding that if the preparations have been made, then the fulfillment of the task will have

inherent in it a certain rhythm and completeness, because the relationships out of which that fulfillment springs have a completeness and a rhythm to them. If the preparations are proper, you ultimately let go. That's exactly what an athlete does. An athlete, you know, runs the plays again and again, so that at the moment of performance, he will be free to take in whatever is happening, and make his moves accordingly. That's also true with performances—or it ought to be.

Design should be worked out the same way. A really good carpenter like Jerry Powell, for example, comes in and says, "Let's move this out a little bit here, because we found something new." I usually say, "Move it out." It's not inspiration, it's not chaos, it's just being prepared. When the performers work in the space with the environmentalist, even more changes occur.

BMc: In a sense, then, the environment only comes to exist in performance, which is not true of a conventional stage setting.

RS: Correct. And it continues to change all during a run. In the various photographs of the environments we're showing only moments, just as if we were to take snapshots of your life. The performance has a life, it is only possible to show different moments in that life. Any one of them can be beautiful but none of them is complete.

BMc: Let me go back to what I asked Jerry before. How did you add or subtract things during the course of the run of *Dionysus?*

JR: One change came when *Dionysus* became a hit. We wanted more audiences, and that was why the north wall unit was built.

BMc: Will you describe it?

JR: The unit was about 30' wide by 19' tall, by 3' deep. It was a sheer wall similar to a huge bookcase with 3' increments through which the spectators snaked their way on different levels. It was very symmetrical and it was built with the same motifs and the same construction methods as the towers.

BMc: What else was added to the environment during the run?

JR: There were two other towers added, one in the southwest corner, and one near the front door at the northeast corner. They were built with diagonal braces, and that bothered my sense of unity. One of the things about the two original towers was that there was no need for such braces; they were constructed so that they couldn't shift off the perpendicular because of the way the "mezzanines" were built in. The "mezzanines" provided a kind of bracing technique, that kept the towers rigid. It is interesting that it was only after a year's run that those original towers became rickety—and only then because the bolts wore against the lumber.

BMc: The mezzanines, so-called, were simply platforms suspended inside the towers. Richard has said that he doesn't believe in accidents. I tend to believe you when you say that the north wall was a structure created to house more people because more people were coming to see the show. But I also don't believe that it was just that, either. It seems that in the course of storing people in the towers something else developed—a new use for the room, a new way of splitting it up between actors and spectators. It seems that in *Dionysus* the whole basis of a new kind of shared space really began to develop out of a relationship between mats and the towers and the other additions. Can you comment on that?

JR: Of all the productions that we have done, I think that *Dionysus* probably had the most audience involvement. The fact that there was relatively little architecture lent itself to dancing, for example, because it provided an open floor space and a kind of promenade for walking. I always believe that people position themselves in accordance with whether they want to be involved or want to be safe. In *Dionysus* people would go to the top of the towers or into the corners because they wanted to remain safe as spectators. But some who wanted to involve themselves would stay on the floor, walk, prowl around, stand up, and move—and therefore they realized that they could begin to dance themselves when the dancing began among the performers. I think that the adding of the bookcase seating was just a further development of that whole process of discovering that space. We started with two towers and then we added other things to get the relationship to develop. It was the production itself that discovered those new things.

RS: There was something else going on, too. As the play became more public, as it became a hit, it became necessary to make more of a division between performance space, observation space, and, something new that came in—private space. When we were doing open rehearsals in May and during the first part of the run, in June and July, 1968, it was a fairly successful production, but it wasn't a great hit. When the play reopened in October, it got a lot of notoriety because of its nakedness. There was no nakedness in *Dionysus* until December, 1968. Occasionally, a woman went topless during the dance section, but the birth and death rituals were done with women in black tights and the men in black jock-straps, so while it was sexy, it didn't have total nakedness. But with the nakedness we got a different kind of audience, some of it an older audience. It was then that the spaces became both public and private. Places were developed where the performers could go and be away from the performance. And there were places where spectators could go and be away from the performance. Under the southwest corner construction, for example, lots of little scenes were played out. You could go underneath that construction and be out of everyone's sight. It was a space maybe 15' or 20' square, where several platforms were pushed together. I recall that we began to aggreggate the platforms as time went on to make a bigger space, and I remember one evening when Bill Finley, a spectator, and I carried on quite a make-out session there. And other things went on back there, too. People would go there to rest. Or when we said we were going to kill Pentheus, performers would hide back there, and some of the dances began back there.

When we began *Dionysus* I was much less radical about costume. I felt that you get a designer who designs costumes, which are special clothes you wear for a performance. So I said, "what would make the women in the play look sexy?" And Ciel Smith came up with the idea of chitons of red without any bras underneath, and black panties. They were sexy. And the men wore black jock straps underneath short pants and T-shirts, or they went bare-chested. When the time came for the birth and death rituals, the men stripped down to their jock straps. It was sexy and effective. But it was weird as I watched it, because somehow, I felt that the women's costumes were out of a college production of a Greek play. Actually, you couldn't get away with that kind of costuming then at most colleges.

Then, we decided to do the birth and death rituals naked—the first naked performance was December 4, 1968. The play began in the street—the first part of *Dionysus* was waiting in the street to get in. Spectators were admitted one at a time, and if you came with someone, you were separated. People sometimes said, "I won't be separated from my date." And I said, "If you won't be

Pentheus (Richard Dia) points out Dionysus (William Finley) in the midst of the crowd. One of the two main towers, used for both audience and performers, is at right of photograph. Photo: Fred Eberstadt

separated from your date, go to a movie." In fact, if there was a large party, I would pick one from the party, then somebody from the end of the line, and then somebody from the middle. The point was, you wait in line, but the *Dionysus* world isn't fair, so maybe the person in back goes in first. Who says that waiting in line means that the first person goes in first? Also the "Dionysian rites" work best on one person at a time. So, out there in the street we had 200 people and the line went all the way up the street because getting into the theatre took a long time, maybe three-quarters of an hour. I began to feel that the performers should be in their regular street clothes so they wouldn't look different from those who arrived to see them. In December we began to wear whatever clothes we were coming to the theatre in. But this developed into a kind of costuming. For example, Joan always wore a certain pair of pants. Others wore the same clothes. The clothes got bloody, and when they got too bad, the theatre gave money to buy some more. These costumes were regular clothes that people bought in a store.

Many people came to watch the *Dionysus* peep show; some came because it was stylish; a lot of people, especially young people, came because they thought it was religion, and thought we believed in it that way. As audiences projected a religion on us, some in the Group began to wonder whether it wasn't religion: "Maybe we're not The Performance Group; maybe we're the Dionysus People." I'm a skeptic and I began to fight against the Dionysus religion. We had struggles about whether we were a theatre or a commune and the seeds of the destruction of that first group, which came about a year later, were sown then. All these things changed the space.

BMc: So the idea of a complex theatrical landscape—which is very much associated with your work, and with Jerry's work, and with the whole environmental idea—really began with

Dionysus. You developed a complex topography, shared by actors and spectators.

RS: You might say that *Victims of Duty*, done the year before, was the inner landscape of Paul Epstein, Franklin Adams, and Richard Schechner. It was our dream landscape. But the *Dionysus* environment became the dream landscape of the performers and the audience, and Jerry and I were midwives to its birth. It relates to gestalt psychotherapy. Fritz Perls writes that all of the images in dreams really represent extensions and projections of the body. In the same way, the space for *Dionysus* was a kind of projection of the relationships between the bodies of the performers and those of the spectators in a dream landscape.

BMc: When *Dionysus* went on, nobody had ever really been involved in a similar environmental situation. What was the response to the fact that some people couldn't see some events, that spectators were uncomfortable, that they couldn't hear some scenes, that the kind of physical relationships which they understood in the theatres had been fractured, destroyed, and reassembled?

RS: It is true that some scenes could not be heard by everyone, such as the first scene between Tiresius and Cadmus. But the scene was played four or five times so everybody could hear it at one time or another, in one place or another. They might play the scene near you, so you would hear it. But you would see that same scene going on somewhere else a few minutes later and you couldn't hear it. Several other scenes were private—certain dances, for example, which you could see only from a distance. And there was a scene where we whispered to individual audience members, "We're going to kill Pentheus in ten minutes. Will you help?" About two thirds of the audience had

Dionysus (William Finley) standing on the tower, curses the Thebans as they clean up the blood from their bodies and the floor. Photo: Fred Eberstadt

that whispered to them. There were chorus fragments where you might not hear the fragment spoken to a person down the line, but you heard other phrases spoken around you. People expect that everyone will hear the same things. Orthodox theatrical design says that there are good seats somewhere, and everything is measured in terms of these good seats. A bad seat is one where the sound or sight is distorted or blocked. In *Dionysus,* and in the later work too, there are no good or bad places. As the action moves the quality of the vantage points change. That's very upsetting because the spectator and the performer don't know from where a scene is going to be played or seen. From one part of the room it's a very bad scene; for another person elsewhere, it's a very good scene. What environmental theatre does is throw back to the spectator the job that the orthodox architect—and the critic—have always done for the spectator. When you walk into a conventional theatre, you already know from experience where the best seat is; you can bitch that you're not there or be happy that you are there, but you know. There is that security. Going into a theatre like the Garage, there is no security.

BMc: The designer in the proscenium theatre orients himself to that best seat, too. The perspective of a box setting is developed from that position; I was taught to paint scenery for someone who sits halfway back in the house.

RS: In the environment of *Dionysus* the spectator and performer are literally in the same interior space. Certain actions were closer and other actions farther away from any given spectator. Some people get upset by this—critics especially. It takes away their precious "objectivity"; they don't know how to evaluate the performance because there would have to be about 15 of them to really explore the space simultaneously. Unfortunately, they don't ask reviewers to explore different aspects of the performance. And most reviewers—John Lahr is a happy exception—stay rooted in one place—in terror or stubborness. No one asked: How was *Dionysus in 69* from the towers; how was it wandering around on the floor; how was it back underneath the platforms—around on the floor? Criticism of environmental theatre ought to be as multi-focused as the theatrical event itself. Spectators threw themselves into *Dionysus*. That kind of involvement can be objective, but it is an objectivity in which you move from point to point and find new perspectives each moment. The "new journalism" of Tom Wolfe and his followers applies that idea of objectivity. To be objective does not mean to be static. After all, the interior logic of *The Bacchae*, from which *Dionysys in 69* was made, is dizzy—a vertigo, the madness of not getting your bearings until after the   deed is done.

BMc: Most of us are tied into the Renaissance theatre tradition of placing ourselves in an auditorium and relating to a perspective visit in front of us. Yet, walking around on a carnival midway, we make choices very easily: this booth, then that booth, then the Ferris wheel, and so on. At the carnival we are able to deal very easily with conflicting sights and sounds, partial sight, partial hearing. In a theatre situation, however, we can't because we've been brought up in that highly focused perspective situation, in which the orientation is to a hypothetical point in space directly in front of us. Even thrust and arena stages demand a single focus. All the important choices have already been made.

RS: You've said that you feel that the avant garde of the last 10 years or so has ended, and I agree. Certainly, a phase of it has ended. But I know that, if nothing else, the Renaissance idea of theatre space is not viable—one can have a number of vantage points, and that scenography is not a setting for the play, but a version of the play.

BMc: It's not so much that the perspective idea is not viable, it's just that there are now perfectly viable alternatives.

RS: I think the perspective concept is no longer viable. A world in which the media is so important, a world of rapid transport, a world of new perceptions, cannot depend on the settled view implied by perspective. If we have quantum mechanics and indeterminacy in physics, quasars and black holes in astronomy, nuclear fusion and fission, DNA and RNA in genetics, then certainly we need multiple viewpoints in theatre architecture if the art is to keep in touch with the rest of society. Environmental theatre is a version of pluralism and indeterminacy.

JR: Richard's "Six Axioms for Environmental Theatre" talks about single focus and multi-focus. Each production places emphasis on one of these. The orthodox theatre depends solely on single focus, but in environmental theatre focus changes at different moments in the play. *Dionysus* is a world of madness, sexuality, ecstasy. And when there's a bacchic dance going on, focus ought to be multiple, but when Pentheus is performing it ought to be single focus. Pentheus is a man who likes to look at his body, he likes to see his body on a tightwire, and everybody's eyes ought to be on him when he scales the tower. Everybody ought to see him when he flings himself into the middle of a scene. So focus changes from moment to moment.

BMc: An indication of how you, Jerry, have abandoned the perspective tradition is that in all your work I've only seen one **drawing** for an environment. I've **seen** models of everything, and ground plans. I suppose that's because it's really impossible to render one of your environments straight on as one would with a conventional stage setting. The only real way to see it, in

miniature, is looking down into a model, walking around and looking first at one part, and then another, and still another part, literally traversing the model as you explore it, rather than trying to deal with it all from a fixed point.

JR: I don't know whether it's true, but I've read that although there was an architectural plan for medieval cathedrals, there were embroideries and embellishments on that plan which came out of the individual craftsmen who followed it. Perhaps, it was because medieval life was more communal and they were more able to accept irregularities; cathedrals were not built exactly symmetrically; there are countless little irregularities, nooks and crannies.

RS: Similarly, in environmental work you talk to the carpenter, who's doing it and say, "Lets put a little bit in here." So he puts a little bit in there.

BMc: How was light used in *Dionysus*?

RS: It was white light all the way, except for a few red gels. Viki May Stang, the stage manager, wanted red gels for the dancing scenes. She thought they would add mood. I don't like to impose my will gratuitously; I'll manipulate, I'll try to convince, I'll do what I can. But she wanted her red gels; that was more important to me than the fact that I didn't want them. So we had three or four red gels, which I disliked at the beginning, I disliked at the middle, and I disliked at the end.

BMc: Why white light?

JR: There is a myth about color; many design text books give you this thing about the face having to be lit amber, and so on. Traditionally in the theatre they have added all sorts of colors to achieve color. But incandescent light is already very amber. And very warm compared to sunlight. The most beautiful way to see human flesh, from my point of view, is under so-called white light, which isn't really white. The stage manager was brainwashed into thinking that color should be added, but it was already there.

BMc: Doesn't this also involve a position about artifice?

RS: I despise colored light and a dim stage. I want to see what's going on. I get nothing out of colored light and dimness except a headache and a squint. In *Dionysus* I wanted the birth and death to take place on an operating table, under the brightest possible light. In our other plays, too, we use bright white light. For *Commune* we turned on everything we had. In *The Tooth of Crime* the lights change as we change scenes, but wherever the scene is, it's bright. *Courage* is like *Commune. Makbeth* is different—with scattered lights, patches of darkness—flashes, sharp beams, shadows, glare.

JR: There's another thing. What a gel does, of course, is to subtract colors from faces and add other colors. I remember working in summer stock situations where aged actresses would come in wanting to look younger. Consequently, they always wanted more pink on their faces. Well, not only did the pink make them look younger, it took out all the other colors and just turned them pink, and suddenly the reality was gone.

RS: I like the environment to be lit so that you see a pool of light on the floor, or light on a tower. Then I ask the actors to seek out the light, rather than waiting until the action is completed and lighting the actors. The lighting is organic to the space, and the action develops in terms of the space. Also that way, sometimes, the face and hands, which are usually lit, are not lit. Who is to say that a hip is less important than the face or hands, that acting is done only with the face or hands? It's done with the entire body, and at certain times, if you have a fragment of light falling on a

Dionysus (Joan MacIntosh) curses the Thebans. Photo: Fred Eberstadt

knee you might find something very expressive which otherwise you might never see.

BMc: Which brings up a question of how you decide to light the space. On what grounds do you make that decision to put a light here but not one there?

RS: On different grounds. I want to have a certain place brightly lit, because the scenes are there. But that's not the only reason. A particular piece of space demands light because it is spatially important and it draws scenes to it. Some lights are used because there is an important scene that attracts light; at other times lights attract a scene. It can happen both ways—and does. Also I like to light the audience, to put them in the show.

DIONYSUS IN 69

By the Performance Group based on Euripides'
The Bacchae
Translated by William Arrowsmith
Music by The Performance Group
Environment by Richard Schechner and Jerry N. Rojo
Directed by Richard Schechner
Opened June 6, 1968

Remi Barclay Agave, Chorus, Messenger
Samuel Blazer Chorus, Coryphaeus, Messenger
Jason Bosseau Chorus, Coryphaeus, Dionysus,
                  Messenger
Richard Dia Cadmus, Chorus, Coryphaeus,
                  Pentheus
William Finley Cadmus, Chorus, Dionysus
Joan MacIntosh Agave, Chorus, Dionysus
Patrick McDermott Chorus, Coryphaeus, Dionysus,
                  Messenger, Tiresias
Margaret Ryan Agave, Chorus
William Shephard Cadmus, Chorus, Pentheus
Ciel Smith Agave, Chorus, Tiresias

Note: In *Dionysus in 69* roles were rotated over the
        run; no one played more than the Chorus and
        one role on any given performance.

11 Makbeth

The Performance Group's second production, *Makbeth* (November 1969-January 1970) used two separate and distinct environments. Upstairs, a long dark tunnel filled with mirrors and graffiti, designed by Brooks McNamara, through which spectators entered The Performing Space, and a multi-level complex of ladders, stairs, and towers, by Jerry Rojo, which occupied the downstairs performing space at the Garage. The technical director was Ed Madden. Unlike the earlier *Dionysus in 69*, spectators remained stationary during the production, the performers moving freely throughout the space.

RS: The *Makbeth* environment was built while The Performance Group was in Yugoslavia. We stopped working in New York at the end of July, 1969; we rehearsed *Makbeth* in Yugoslavia in September. When we returned to New York in mid-October, the environment was built. Of course, the basic ideas for the space came from workshops we ran two or three times a week from about December, 1968—*Dionysus* was in the midst of its run then—through until July of 1969. You two were not involved until late winter. The first workshops consisted of taking Shakespeare's script apart and putting it back together in new ways.

BMc: What did you do with the script?

RS: We made a series of short scenes that occurred in bursts, so that occasionally three or four scenes took place simultaneously. Then a couple of more scenes would happen. The play required spaces for scenes to occur simultaneously. And it needed one central playing area. The language was absolutely Shakespeare's—we used only his words, but the play and the story were restructured.

BMc: Jerry, what was the early plan for the space?

JR: The three of us were talking about spaces and images.

Brooks drew a ziggurat—actually an inverted ziggurat.

BMc: Or, to say it another way, it was using a ziggurat as negative space inside the structure—that is, there were a series of chambers around a hollow space; then above them was another row of chambers which hung out over the first, rather like the upper stories of a medieval house; the third story hung out over the second, and so on, so that the space became, as it got higher, increasingly confined. It seems to me that the ziggurat idea, or something stemming from it, is involved in Jerry's designs for the Manhattan Project's *Endgame*.

JR: Some interesting notions came out of it—for example, the effect might be rather like an operating theatre with an audience of medical students, or the floor could be sand or dirt, like a bullfight or gladiatorial arena.

BMc: Another idea which was also fed in and ultimately influenced the *Makbeth* design, was one for which I built a model. It stemmed from designs I did for a production of Kenneth Brown's *The Brig*. The idea was to create a metal cityscape in which people were confined in very small cages or cabins. These cabins were to be like the rooms in buildings. The corridors were, in effect, city streets, and the action was to take place in the streets, in some of the rooms, and so on. The premise was to create a cityscape topography filled with small areas in which the actors could perform, in some cases without being completely seen or heard by the spectators who were to be placed in little cabins around the room. Both of these concepts—the ziggurat and the cityscape—fed into Jerry's environment, which covered the entire first floor of The Performing Garage. I eventually created a second environment—a maze covering a portion of the second floor—which we will talk about later.

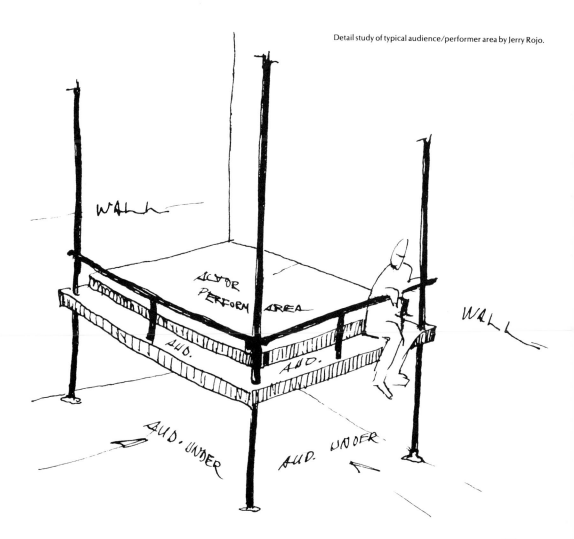

Detail study of typical audience/performer area by Jerry Rojo.

RS: Hearing some of these ideas now, I wish we had used them, especially the idea of the ziggurat and the dirt floor. The idea of the bullfight arena or the slaughterhouse appeals to me very much, too. I think I like the idea of sawdust because it's cleaner than dirt and because it has a certain kind of feeling that I like—both circus and slaughterhouse. I still would like to do an environment which combined bullring, slaughterhouse, and operating room.

The reason we moved way from some of these ideas was my conservatism; I felt ultimately that we needed a central playing space. I was scared of a really fragmented space. My concern about fire laws drew me away from audience cubicles because I felt that we just wouldn't get them approved. Another pressure was that we had to think how to get 200 people in. We couldn't afford an environment like the one for Grotowski's *Faustus*, where he let only 40 people in.

BMc: On the average, how many people have you seated in the various environments at the Garage?

RS: *Dionysus* ranged from 175 to 250. When we were closing, and we wanted to pack them in, there was one horrendous night when we had nearly 400 people in there. For *Makbeth*, the most we had was about 220. It could comfortably hold 150. In terms of actual business, because it was murdered by the critics—especially Walter Kerr—there was an average of around 50 or 60. For *Commune* we had up to 230 people, but it averaged around 145, and often as few as 25. *The Tooth of Crime*, with its free standing center environment and *Mother Courage*, are the smallest, no more than 175 spectators.

BMc: For the *Makbeth* production, spectators entered the Garage by a small door on Wooster Street, and found themselves on a steep flight of stairs leading to the second floor. On the second floor spectators walked into a long rectangular black room, hung up their coats, and proceeded through the maze which led spectators to a trapdoor in the floor—the one we've mentioned earlier—and down a winding staircase into Jerry's environment. Interestingly, the effect was not that of simply walking downstairs to the first floor from the second floor, but of going from a first floor into a gigantic subterranean chamber, a huge white basement.

The maze was designed to introduce the spectator to the nature of the performance, that fragmented quality about which we've talked, through a combination of graphic materials involved with past productions of *Macbeth* and the present production. It was a kind of collage, a physical arrangement that mirrored the complexity and fragmentation central to the play. One image I used as a reference point for the maze was the Chamber of Horrors at Madame Tussaud's with its irregular lighting which constantly changes in intensity, causing you to bump into the wax figures. After a while you are unable to determine whether a wax figure is a wax figure or a human being. I also borrowed an image from the carnival tradition—the glass house or hall of mirrors, in which you move through, inch-by-inch, feeling your way because it's unclear whether any wall is a mirror, or a sheet of glass, or a door leading into another chamber. Spectators moved through the maze, feeling their way, bumping into mirrors, seeing themselves, seeing other spectators, and seeing blowups of characters from *Makbeth*. This was, in part, because the maze was intentionally very dark, narrow, confined, and difficult to maneuver in. When a spectator got to the end of the maze, and began to descend the stairs into the main environment, all of a sudden he was confronted with a gigantic bright space, and the contrast was startling.

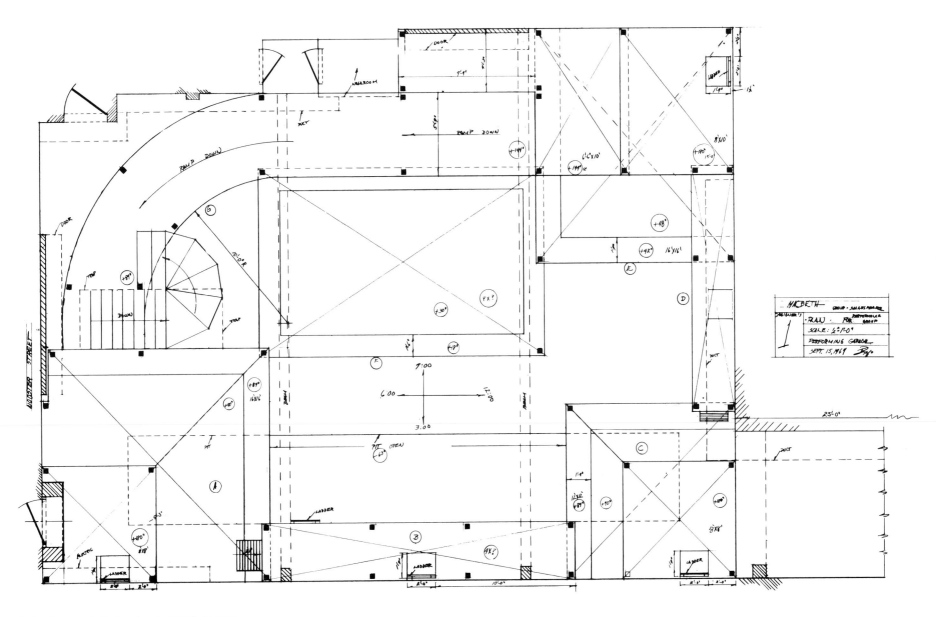

Designer's ground plan for the main environment by Jerry Rojo.

JR: The maze provided a historical analogue, as well as feeding all of our notions about *Makbeth*—that gothic, dark, secret, medieval feeling that is in the play, the sense of crime and punishment, guilt and horror. The downstairs environment was a contrast. I felt that I had never constructed anything so immense, and I think that it may have been the first time that an environment was constructed on such a prodigious scale. I think that it was one of the real breakthroughs in this kind of work—for the first time a production confronted the audience in a massive, total way, far more so than in *Dionysus*. I think there was more participation in *Dionysus* in a physical, tactile way, but *Makbeth* was the first time that an audience really lived in the same house with the play and had a sense of total space.

BMc: *Makbeth* represents the first example of a very complex terrain inside The Performing Garage; it was far more complex than *Dionysus* in terms of levels, performing spaces, audience space, and so on, although the seeds of that complexity were apparent in the way the towers, mats, and auxiliary towers were used in *Dionysus*.

JR: I might say, in retrospect, that the experience of building the environment was terrifying. My last day in New York, Richard still hadn't decided whether he was going to build it or not. The Performance Group was off to Europe. We had a final meeting and he said, "Okay, Jerry, build it." So the Group went, leaving me with a $15,000 to $20,000 project. There were questions about zoning, audience, safety codes; all these immense problems which nobody had ever really confronted before in the garage and Richard wasn't going to be around to say what we should or should not do. But it was also good to be able to build it in complete freedom. It was good to go into the Garage with a model and literally transform that scale model into an actual environment. When Richard and the Group came back from Europe they were awestruck because they were used to looking at the model. The difference was comparable to being in an eight story building and looking down into the street and then suddenly actually walking in the street. It was a terrifying experience for the whole Group.

RS: We never before—or since—came into a finished space that way. Our workshops gave us an idea but no real experience of the space. In *Environmental Theater* I talk about the difficulties of rehearsing in one kind of space—as we did in a meadow in Baocic, Yugoslavia—and ultimately doing the play in a completely different kind of space in the Garage. It was a contradiction that the production never recovered from.

BMc: What did the spectator see as he began to come down the stairs from the maze to the main environment?

JR: Well, basically you came down the stairs onto a huge wooden structure: the vertical supporting members were 4" by 4" with 2" by 6" framing members, ¾" plywood as surface material, and handrails and ladders made of ¾" steel pipe. As you descended the stairs you had more than a three-quarter view of the space. Every spectator who came into the space was immediately visible to everyone else—you could only enter one at a time because of the narrowness of the stairs—so that as each spectator came down he was scrutinized by the entire audience. Thus, there was a one-to-one introduction of each spectator into the space. Then you went down to another level, the second level from the floor, where you had a choice of going on to a large ramp on the left, south wall, or to the right, onto one of the main corner platform playing areas which led to a gallery on the north wall. Or, if you chose, you could continue on down the spiral staircase to the main floor, where

you could move to the right underneath a tower, to the left underneath the ramp, or you could walk onto the "table," which was the center playing area. The table was high with a bench on all four sides, and it was interlocked with a two-storied, tower-like structure on the southwest corner. Then there were towers on the northeast and northwest corners. There were three main towers all interlocked so that the whole structure was tied together. On each tower there was a ladder, which enabled the audience and performers to climb up through a trapdoor. When you had climbed the ladder of the northwest tower, for example, you came out onto a second level, which was a 16′ square playing area, with audience seated on two sides of it. At this level there was another ladder leading to a second platform above, which was smaller. The audience could sit on two sides of it, dangling their feet down over the platform just below. This top story provided very private places for the performers.

This environment served as a basis for the University of Connecticut Mobius Theatre, the Sarah Lawrence Theatre, and other projects. This happens often. A production or a concept triggers variations. *Makbeth* was an original, but the concept is serviceable and people can use it in a wide range of ways.

BMc: How was the environment shared by actors and spectators? What was the flow of performance? Who owned what terrains and how did the nature of the space shift?

RS: First of all, there were four categories of performers in the play. There were *The Doers*, who were Makbeth and Lady Makbeth. There were *The Avengers*, Malcolm and MacDuff, who avenged the murders of *The Founders*, or *Victims*, who were Duncan and Banquo. And there were *The Dark Powers*, who were the Three Witches, but also all the lesser characters —messengers, soldiers, and the minor kinsmen and nobles —

Lady Makbeth (Priscilla Smith) contemplates Makbeth's letter. Note the blackened audience seating area in relation to performance space. Photo: Fred Eberstadt

Makbeth (William Finley) orders two of the Dark Powers to murder Banquo.
Photo: Fred Eberstadt

the common people who hate the aristocrats. Each had a terrain. For example, the Makbeths owned the center table, more or less, and controlled it; but it was also a battlefield and they were losing it bit by bit. The tower in the southwest, the largest tower area, also belonged to the Makbeths, it was Inverness and later Dunsinane. Duncan and Banquo were identified with the tower in the northeast, a smaller tower, but still the second largest one. That's where the play begins. When Duncan comes to Inverness the night he is murdered—that's where his bed is. The coronation of Makbeth takes place there because Makbeth replaces Duncan. Immediately Makbeth orders Banquo killed, and Banquo is killed on the ground floor, underneath this tower where the king stands.

BMc: Then it's not that each category of performer was necessarily limited to a certain space; it's just that each had a particular place with which he was associated.

RS: Right, each had a different house or station. In every play I direct, characters get identified with places in the environment. It helps the audience, and it helps the performer even more. Even if it doesn't help them, it sure as hell helps me. I do the blocking and I'm very territorial.

The Avengers—Malcolm and MacDuff—start with no space at all. They're the only ones who enter down the stairway. They are the kids. I grew up in a family of four sons and I adapted the play so that it was about five sons (one of them, Cawdor, is killed and is never seen). As soon as Malcolm and MacDuff come down the stairs they step onto the table, which is a kind of public place, and begin to fight with each other. When Duncan goes to sleep they go to sleep in a tower right above him. They watch the murder. They encourage it. They laugh above it. But, they're squeezed way up near the ceiling. Still later Duncan's

funeral procession moves up the ramp and Duncan is laid into a kind of coffin at the edge with his head hanging down in a net bag. There was a hole cut in the floor and Duncan lay back with his head hanging down into the first level and the audience sitting below saw it in the bag. It was uncomfortable, but he had to stay there for the rest of the play because he had lines after death. Duncan, and later Banquo, too, became a chorus cursing the Makbeths. Anyway, the Avengers start up the ramp. Their job is to move from the southwest corner, back down across the ramp, to the northeast corner, gather their forces, and then out across the table for the final attack on Dunsinane. Finally, when Makbeth is killed, the Avengers take over the table, briefly. Then Malcolm orders MacDuff killed, Malcolm is alone with the crown, and the last thing we see him do is go back up the stairs, biting on the crown. He is trying to consume, to internalize, the power as he is being forced out of the space. As he leaves the Dark Powers occupy the table.

The Dark Powers know all the secret spaces. They could get from any one space to any other without being seen. The Dark Powers are identified with the open pit, which is 40' long and 8' wide and 7' deep. The play begins with the Dark Powers sitting in the bottom of the pit. While speaking, the Dark Powers move from the pit up to the highest part of the space—it takes about five minutes—where they transform into gargoyles peering into the room. The Dark Powers control the corners, the high spots, and the low spots. They never enter the center except as servants, and at the very end. Near the end of the play Lady Makbeth commits suicide and her corpse lies in Dunsinane. Makbeth's corpse is lying close to her. Duncan is lying in his grave. Banquo is lying over by the door in the northeast corner. MacDuff is lying in the northwest corner. There's a line spoken by a Dark Power: "The rich warring against the rich, the great nobles tearing each other to pieces—it cannot be soon enough for me! Are these noble nobles fit to govern? No, not fit to live!" And they don't. Malcolm is the only one left. He exits up the stairs; the Dark Powers jump onto the table, sprawl out there. At last they control the table. "How will you live?" "As the birds to." "What, with worms and flies?" "With what I get. So pray you, remember the porter." So the play ends.

Neither *Dionysus* nor *Makbeth* had an intermission. *Dionysus* went on about two and a half hours without intermission, but within it there were great breathing spaces, like intermissions while the play was going on. The same principle was used in *Commune. Makbeth* had no intermission, and it was intense, but it only went on for an hour and ten minutes. *Dionysus* began before the audience came in, so that spectators entered an already live environment, where the performers were doing exercises and sounds were being made. In *Makbeth*, we did it two ways: during part of the run, the performers were sitting slumped against the posts, as though they were sleeping when the audience entered; but most of the run, the performers were in the back room in the northwest corner. The audience came into the space completely alone—no ushers, no programs. In *Dionysus* somebody said, "Good evening, sir, may I take you to your seat?" There was the illusion that maybe somebody would help you. In *Makbeth*, there was no introductory stuff. When it came time for the play to begin, the stage manager came out and rapped a big stick, as they do in the French theatre, ten times. Then the actors screamed, came out at a half-trot, as at a football game, and took different positions in a tableaux. Duncan, MacDuff, Malcolm, and Banquo were in a grouping. Makbeth was alone in another place, and Lady Makbeth was between the two towers reciting Makbeth's letter to herself. Then in a series of stop-actions, the

performers would move from freeze to freeze, as the Dark Powers were reciting their lines. While the Dark Powers recited their incantation, the others, frame by frame, moved into position for the first scene. That introduction was startling. At the finish of the play—an hour and ten minute rush—it was breathless—there was a sudden blackout. The performers fled from the space. The lights came on again and the theatre was empty except for spectators. It was dreamlike.

BMc: To what extent is the environment shared with the audience?

RS: I didn't want free movement of audience. One night I asked them to move around, following the action. My request came from desperation, because we had so few spectators. When the house was full, I was happy if people sat absolutely still. To mark out where spectators could sit, we tacked down 2' wide rug runners around the edges of the performer's spaces. The audience filled the edges of the spaces. Actions took place behind them, underneath them, or in another part of the room, as well as in front of them.

BMc: So a mobile audience isn't necessarily a canon in your work. I think a number of people believe that it is.

RS: No, definitely not. I've used a mobile audience only in *The Tooth of Crime.* In *Dionysus, Commune,* and *Mother Courage* the audience can move, but it's not basically a mobile audience. In *Makbeth*, definitely, the audience was fixed, rooted, trapped. I wanted them to experience sounds and sights out of their line of vision. You looked across at another spectator and said, "He's seeing what's going on but I can't see it." That frustration was part of the conspiracy and brutality at **the heart of the** production.

BMc: Did the spectators occupy some of the same places occupied by the actors?

RS: No. The spectators were on the edges of platforms, and the performers were in the center of those platforms. No spectator was allowed on the central table; they sat around it. From one point of view, the spectators surrounded the performers and trapped them; from another point of view, the performers surrounded the spectators. Everybody was trapped. The space reeked with rage, hostility, brutality. We took out most of the rugs—the floor was bare cold cement. The performers wore boxing shoes. The lighting was glaring, intentionally focused into the spectators' eyes, alternating with total darkness. The production had treacherous creases and dangerous corners. It was not comfortable for us or for the audience. Maybe that was why so few came to see it. Another thing was that *Makbeth* was the only play The Performance Group did that ran only in winter. It opened in November and closed at the end of January. Because of the lousy heating in the Garage it got very cold. The rugs of *Dionysus* insulated the Garage; also *Dionysus* began in the summer and the whole feel of the summer carried through. *Makbeth*, on the other hand, was a winter of discontent play. It ran through half of a very bitter winter with a lot of snow, and it ended when the Group exploded and split in the middle of that winter. So, it was not only a white, bright hell, but a cold hell. The whole feeling of the Garage changes radically between seasons. We shouldn't ignore that. Part of me wants better heating and better air-conditioning; another part likes changes in response to the outside. If the city is sweltering, the theatre is sweltering. If the city is freezing, the theatre is freezing. It s rhythm is tied to the rhythm of the city. In *Mother Courage*, a play whose cruelty matches *Makbeth's* scene 9 is played in Wooster Street in front of the Garage, and scenes 10, 11, and 12 in the Garage with the big overhead door open. The street's weather and rhythms come into the theatre—and the theatre spills into the street.

BMc: The actual materials used in the *Makbeth* environment were essentially the same as those used in *Dionysus*?

RS: The feeling was utterly different because of the metal railings on the towers and pit, the cement floor, the bare walls, the many sharp corners and steep drops, the open pit.

BMc: Can you contrast the feeling of the two?

RS: In *Dionysus* we had 200 people each performance. A lot of them sat on the floor, sometimes eight or ten rows deep; or they stood clumped together, the colors of their clothes creating a kind of bright wash. In *Makbeth*, on the other hand, the audience was a single line of people in a cold white room under fierce lighting. In *Dionysus* the lighting faded in and out, but in *Makbeth* it was turn on, turn off.

JR: There is a suggestion that the downstairs environment is a castle. There's a kind of main hall and a series of anterooms, chambers, dungeons, and passageways underneath things, and finally, a spiral staircase that seems to lead to a tower. And there were all the hard edges and corners—it was terrifying to come down the very steep and narrow staircase into the room and then to climb a tower on a dangerous hand-over ladder.

BMc: The feeling of great height in the room seemed to be reinforced by the fact that you entered from the top, like going down into a kiva, an Indian ceremonial room. I had the idea to plexiglass a section of the floor of the maze so people could look down into the main environment. The thought was absolutely horrifying. A spectator would think at first that he was stepping into a hole and falling into the main room below.

JR: *Makbeth* is a play about hell and damnation so that walking down into a light, bright hell, where all this is taking place, is an important section. When you're in hell you can go even farther down into the pit, the deepest, most damned place. The space really plumbed that whole linear/vertical structure that is suggested by heavens, gods, devils, purgatory and hell. And it used all the levels of the Garage except the roof.

BMc: As a matter of fact, we thought about using the trapdoor to the roof directly above the trap which led into the main environment. We thought of building another staircase which would lead up through that second trap onto the roof. That would make it possible for a spectator to go through the maze, go up onto the roof, look out over Soho, come down again, and descend all the way down into the lower environment.

We should probably say a word about the use of light. The lighting in the maze was almost non-existent. I began by putting up a number of metal reflector lighting fixtures over mirrored panels so that the light was reflected. First I used 40 watt bulbs, and discovered that they gave too much light. I tried smaller and smaller wattage bulbs, until finally I came up with refrigerator bulbs. What we got then was a pool of light spreading out only a few feet, isolated in the blackness in front of a mirror. Then there was virtual blackness again and then another light. There were no more than four or five refrigerator bulbs down the whole length of this 40' maze. At the end, there were no lights at all, except the light from the environment below shining up through the trap; you had to feel your way to the open floor, and then you went down into the brightly lit environment below.

JR: With some pockets of semi-darkness, we intentionally developed some sense of dimly lit hiding places.

RS: *Makbeth* used the most intricate lighting of any play I'd done until then. The basic image was of flashes of light. The feel of suddeness, storms, and brilliant perception being sunk in darkness. There were more than 50 cues. By contrast, *Commune* had two. In *Makbeth*, action went on in so many different places that the lighting helped the audience to know where to hunt.

JR: Compared to *Dionysus*, there was also a much greater use of steeply angled light. You remember the witches hanging upside down in the pit like bats. There was a light coming up from the pit, and as they swung in and out, the ray of light would make their faces brighter or darker. The movement through the light was important. There was a suggestion of a forest underneath the towers, particularly in the area near the street on the east side of the room. The lights filtering through the vertical posts was very nice.

BMc: What were the costumes like?

JR: They were uniform and unisex. I designed them with Lou Rampino. They were like jump suits, made out of crushed corduroy, with pants like sweatpants. They looked like army fatigues. Everyone wore boxing shoes. They allowed the performers to move easily through the space—as soldiers would, or as killers.

RS: We color-coded them so that the Doers wore a kind of wine or blood-red; the Founders wore off-white; the Avengers wore light chocolate brown; and the Dark Powers wore midnight blue. Consequently, the division of characters was very clear. Except for color, the costumes were identical.

BMc: What is the function of costume in this environment? What are you attempting to do with costume?

RS: The core action of *Makbeth* was a gladiatorial match, or a war. A separation had to be made between the performers and the audience, and among the teams of performers. The costumes told you who the teams were, but they also told you that they were them and you were you. There was no participation in *Makbeth*. In *Dionysus*, by contrast, the performers looked like people off the street. In orthodox theatre, costumes tell the spectator about the character. In *Makbeth* the costumes simply identified four teams and separated all of these teams from the people who were watching. In *Commune, The Tooth of Crime,* and *Mother Courage,* costumes were used in the orthodox way.

BMc: In *Makbeth,* you didn't make content decision with the costumes?

RS: No. We made formal decisions with them, but there was no character costuming.

BMc: What about the function of audience discomfort in all these environments?

RS: It's not discomfort so much as non-comfort. One of the great prejudices of orthodox theatre is the definition of comfort in that peculiar American-automobile idiom—the softer the seat, the plusher the surroundings, the more "comfortable" you are. It's bizarre. The apartments and lofts of some of my friends are comfortable but sparse. The audience is entitled to an experience that is part of the production. If *Makbeth* is "cabin'd, crib'd, and confin'd," then they are

entitled to the "cabin'd, crib'd, and confin'd-ness" of it. How you are, where you are, in what you are, is part of the performance. I can imagine productions where spectators allow body heat, smell, and sweat to affect them as in *Dionysus.* In *Commune,* you might be grouped with three or four others, which is a very comfortable feeling. Or you could lie down on cushioned rugs. Or you might be in an uncomfortably bunched circle. In *Makbeth* spectators were strung out one by one. There might be a person next to you, but you were more isolated than in the orthodox theatre; there was nobody in front of you and nobody behind you. Spectators for *The Tooth of Crime* often stood in a crowd peering over the heads of other people to see a scene, much as they do at a street fight. Or it was like the 1939 New York World's Fair, looking down at a panorama of action.

The supper of *Mother Courage* looked like a picnic on the battlefield—spectators sitting everywhere with trays on the floor or on their legs. Each production generates its own kind of audience arrangement, based not merely on interpretation of the narrative, not only on the story but on the feeling which the story generates, or the feeling which the performers generate—these are the root metaphors of the production. The story and the performers and the space join to birth a metaphor and the audience is part of that metaphor. They not only experience it, they build it, they add to it, they incarnate it. For every spectator, every other spectator is a performer.

JR: People were cliff dwellers at *Commune.* They were in pigeonholes that they had to worm their way up to and then sit or lie or squat, pushed up against somebody else. They smelled all kinds of smells.

RS I find these things comfortable, marvelous. I love to smell people, and be close to them, and touch them.

JR: I have a pet theory about this. I think of the film as totally opposite to this sort of experience. To me, film is essentially a masturbatory, private, personal kind of thing. You go to a movie theatre to be protected; the image is always on a screen; it's safe; it's on celluloid. No matter how horrendous the experience on the screen may seem to be, it's a totally vicarious experience, because that seat is plush, and you're eating popcorn, and there's music. The only possible risk is of the building falling down. But in theatre the exact opposite is true. You don't do what you want to do, you do what the whole congregation wants you to do, you do what the production wants you to do. You're committed to the event in a total sense. I've argued with film people about this. They insist that there is a confrontation going on in film. But we spend hours watching the news because it's safe. We don't have to be over there fighting; we can be sitting on our sofas eating popcorn and watching the Israelis and the Arabs fight. I think that's the difference between theatre and media. I think comfort—physical and emotional comfort, or the lack of it—is right at the center of that difference.

View of the main environment showing the spiral staircase and center performing area/table. Note ramp level on right.

MAKBETH

By William Shakespeare, adapted by Richard Schechner and The Performance Group
Music by Paul Epstein
Costumes by Lewis Rampino and Jerry N. Rojo
Environment by Jerry N. Rojo
Directed by Richard Schechner
Opened November 20, 1969

Jason Bosseau, Richard Dia, Joan MacIntosh Dark Powers
Remi Barclay Banquo
William Finley Makbeth
Tom Crawley Duncan
Stephen Borst Macduff
William Shephard, then **Ernst Shenck,** then **Spalding Gray** Malcolm
Ciel Smith Lady Makbeth

113

12 Commune

The environment for *Commune*, a 1970 production by The Performance Group based on the activities of the Charles Manson Family and American atrocities in Vietnam was designed by Jerry Rojo, with technical direction by Jerry Powell and Barry Klein. In two corners of the space were pueblolike structures of wood, used mainly by the audience, although some performance also took place in these areas. The pueblos were connected by highwaylike galleries which provided elevated passageways around the interior of the room. The concrete floor of the Performing Garage was covered with plywood, and a large plywood "wave" was used as a central performance area.

RS: An important thing happened at the end of *Makbeth*—the Group that made both *Makbeth* and *Dionysus* split up. The only people who continued were Joan MacIntosh, Steve Borst, Spalding Gray (who had come in at the very end of *Makbeth*), and me. With us were Jerry Rojo, of course, and Paul Epstein, both of whom had worked with the Group but weren't into the day-to-day work. We lost control of the Garage in February, 1970. Part of the Group that split from us, led by Patrick McDermott, took over the Garage from February through April. There he produced *The Sorrows of Emer* and *Reynard the Fox* with La Mama ETC and Ciel Smith and Bill Finley. That's when Will Leach worked in our space—maybe that led to the Sarah Lawrence project. Finley, Ciel, and McDermott had all been in The Performance Group, although McDermott wasn't in *Makbeth*. Ciel played Lady and Finley played Makbeth in *Makbeth*.

What they did to the *Makbeth* space for *Emer* and *Reynard* broke my heart. The audience sat along the north wall, though a few of them were seated around the other corners. The whole south wall became a backstage and the *Makbeth* table was used

Ground plan of *Commune* environment by Jerry Rojo.

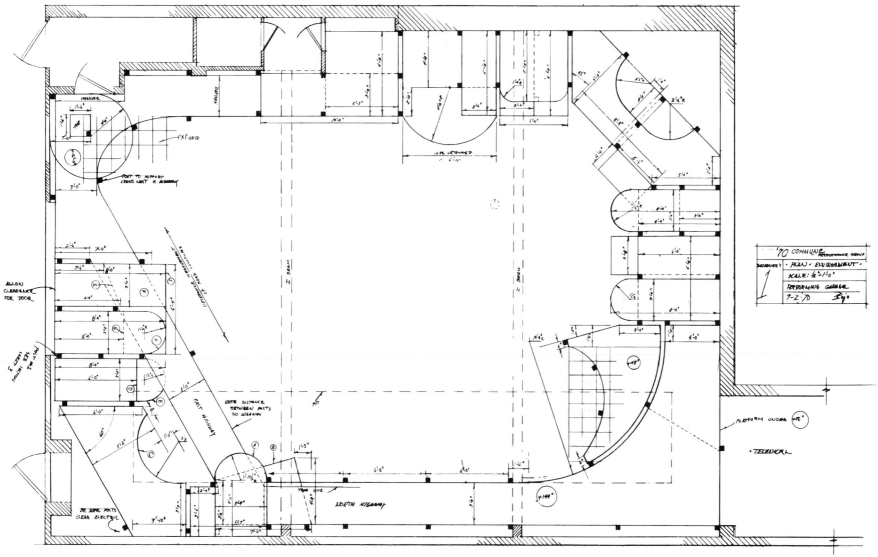

as a thrust stage. Next, Charles Ludlam and the Ridiculous Theatrical Company, whom I admire very much, came in with *Bluebeard*. I'd seen it at Christopher's End, a little bar on Christopher Street. I thought it was a masterpiece. Ludlam was looking for a theatre so I invited him to come down and work in the Garage. In the late spring of 1970, the Ridiculous came in. They set up bridge chairs, and used the space as a proscenium theatre. I admired the play and the Company so much that I didn't mind, even though I don't like to see the Garage used in that way. We reconstituted the Group in the spring of 1970, and began work on *Commune*. We rehearsed next door in Norman Taffel's space, and repossessed the Garage in September, 1970. In the summer of 1970 we went to the State University of New York at New Paltz, where we developed *Commune*. Richard Brown and John Herr brought us there.

Early in the studies for the play I researched pueblos and kivas. We decided that the space should be a terrain—it needed sky, water, hills, plains, and pueblos. Jerry came to New Paltz several times and watched the work. *Commune* was the first work we composed from scratch. We were using materials from American history, the Manson story, and scenes from Shakespeare and Marlowe, but without starting from a given play as we had with *Macbeth* and *The Bacchae*.

Robert Adzema, a sculptor living in New Paltz submitted a model that had an undulating floor. There was no way to build his conception except at an expense beyond our means. But it was from Adzema's idea of a rolling terrain that we came up with the wave. We had to build something for the Garage that would also tour. Jerry solved that problem with his plans for a sectional, modular wave. He also created the ambiance of the environment with curves, ramps, overhangs, diving boards, ellipses, cubbyholes: the pueblo feel. Of all the environments,

I think I love *Commune* the most. It developed organically with the production. The wave was actually built in August in New Paltz. Also in August, we found an old cider still which we cut down to make a 7′ diameter tub, 3′ high. The wave was our terrain and the tub our ocean. Wherever we toured, we took them with us. They were our environmental theatre security blankets, even though a bitch to truck. We took them with us to Goddard College when we were in residence in September, and them brought them to the Garage. Jerry built the other elements of the environment around them. I remember doing lots of rehearsals, and some open rehearsals with the environment partially built. The environment was like a half-built highway that just stopped, blocked off with guard rails so that you couldn't go further and fall off an unfinished ramp.

The staging of *Commune* developed hand-in-hand with the space. It harmonized with the construction of the wave, finding the tub, building the pueblos, and then painting the Garage. It was the first time we used color in the Garage—blue on the ceiling—our sky—and terra-cotta on the walls—our desert. Then we put in the plywood floor which made the room very nice for barefoot movement. We wanted everybody barefoot, but I didn't want rugs. Each of the performers found a different place in the environment for her or his house. The audience sat in groups of five, or six, or in solitary places. They could sit on the floor or they could go high up. It was extraordinarily flexible and beautiful. It was an environment that I wanted to keep in the Garage permanently. That never seems to happen.

BMc: What changes did you make in the Garage for the *Commune* environment? How was the room reconstructed?

JR: As Richard just mentioned, one of the main changes was the new floor. The idea was to get a floor which you could jump

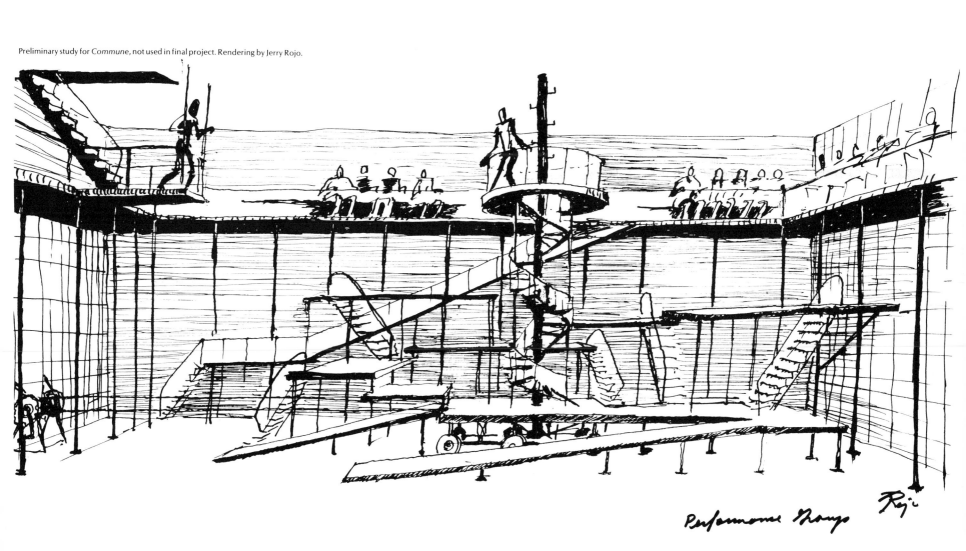

Performance Group   Rojo

Another study, not used. Jerry Rojo

Performance Group   Rojo

on from a high place or which you could dance on. A good dance floor has a lot of resiliency. As a matter of fact, one dance studio in New York City has a wooden floor actually on huge 12″ diameter springs. The ¾″ plywood that we used offers a nice amount of spring, but we knew we also had to support the immense weight of the two pueblos, one in the northeast corner and one in the southwest corner of the room. The pueblos themselves were heavy; and when we added the weight of the audience, the floor had to be tremendously strong.

I also saw the pueblos as ships, in that sailing ships are run essentially as a communal operation, where everybody tows his own weight, does his portion of the work. The whole concept of climbing through the rigging and doing a task was important.

BMc: Describe the pueblos in detail.

JR: The pueblos were constructed from floor to ceiling. They were 19′ tall, about 15′ wide, and 6′ to 8′ deep. Essentially they were made up of small pigeonhole units that you came into by a series of fairly steep ships' ladders. Ordinary steps incline 45 degrees, but ships' ladders can incline 60 degrees or even more. The ships' ladders joined the pigeonholes with other levels which Richard calls diving boards—they were little balconies cantilevered out from the structure.

BMc: How would you contrast the pueblos with the spaces you created for *Makbeth*?

JR: In *Makbeth* there were single lines of audience seated in concentric rings around the performing area. The actors went inside a ring of audience to perform, and they moved from ring to ring through connecting passageways. In *Commune*, the pueblos provided a kind of essential cityscape into which the

audience would climb.

BMc: Was there performing in the pueblos?

JR: Richard has talked about the "houses" that belonged to the performers. Most established their homes in the pueblos— little areas where they kept their clothes and personal belongings. The performers often spoke, sang, or made sounds from the pueblos, to that degree they were used for performing. And there was a lot of climbing up through pueblos and perching on them—Joan did a dive off a pueblo, for example. So, they were used but not in the same sense that they were used in *Makbeth*. I think that the *Commune* environment was essentially an arena. The pueblos and the roads connecting one pueblo to another circled the room. And in the center, on and around the wave, the main performing took place.

BMc: So no major performance took place in the pueblos themselves. They were habitats.

JR: In fact, they were related to Habitat of the Montreal Expo '67, which was part of the inspiration for the pueblos. None of the pigeonholes were set up like windows in a building, arranged one after the other in a symmetrical organization. They were off-center, asymmetrical.

BMc: Basically they ringed the room, with the wave in the center as the central performing space. Were there any other structures in the room?

JR: Off in the northeast corner there was a tall "crows nest," which was part of the whole ship image.

A large tub of water made from the old cider still was also part of the architecture. The wave was constructed with a "hook" on the west end, and in that hook was a kind of inlet, like a cove where the tub was set. The performers used the tub in many ways. It was the Atlantic Ocean; it was the Caribbean; it was blood, and Sharon Tate's swimming pool. Incidentally, we wanted the wave to encompass the entire room, but that was impractical because one of the requirements was that the wave be portable. I tried to design a wave out of wood that could be portable but as large as the performers and crew could possibly handle. The wave turned out to be 24' long and about 12' wide; the back end about 30" high. The way we solved the problem was to first construct a wooden armature out of 2" by 4" framing members. The armature was essentially the section-through of the wave. It was exactly like building a boat. A boat has compound curves to it, and the curve changes at different places. We had about 8 armatures that ran down the length of the wave, and in certain places internally double armatures, curved side to side as well as lengthwise. For the top we had to build to ¾" in order for it to take the amount of weight that it would have to take, so we built up layers of ¼" plywood which could be easily bent. One layer would be put on, nailed and glued, and then another layer would be put on, with overlapping joints, until the whole piece was build up. Once it was finished, it was cut along the double armatures. The wave then came apart in 8 pieces, which were about 8' long, 4' wide, and in different places, some 24" to 30" tall. The elements could then be trucked. Incidentally, there were four more waves built over a two-year period, left in different parts of the world, scattered all over the place.

RS: One was built in Paris, one was built in Poland, one was built for domestic touring, and one was built in California.

BMc: Will you contrast the character of this environment with that of *Makbeth?* What were the principal differences in terms of feeling and quality?

JR: Probably the essential thing was that this was the first time we dealt with curved surfaces. Part of the communal feeling came from the performers flowing into one another, and I think the curving lines suggest that.

RS: The wood floor was important—it was the most important single change. In *Dionysus* there were rugs which burn the skin and are not resilient, so most of the heavy physical action was on the 12' by 16' rectangle of black, hard rubber mats in the center of the space. In *Makbeth,* on the other hand, there was vertical angularity and that cold, stark, cement floor.

Commune was both orthodox and radical. The orthodoxy lay in the fact that it was an arena production, 90% of the audience surrounded the performers, even though they surrounded them in an unusual way. There was a fragment of rug for spectators to sit on in the middle, but they didn't, except when we forced them. During one scene, the telling of the My Lai massacre, we sat spectators in the middle of the wave, but otherwise the audience stayed on the surround. We had much more room to perform in than ever before, and we were able to do certain big movements like the slow–motion race, which began on the southeast side of the room and went two-thirds the way around; or the Tate murder scene, which used all the floor and wave in a complicated balletic way. We even used the pueblos and tub. We couldn't have done that kind of thing in *Makbeth.* There actions fragmented, or were confined. We couldn't have done it in *Dionysus* because the audience was all over the place, and because the rugs didn't permit the precision of movement that is possible on a wood floor.

Commune. The pretty man in the tub. Photo: Elizabeth LeCompte

JR: There's a clear, polyurethane veneer that we've been using a great deal in conjunction with these wood structures; it's very heavy and withstands a tremendous amount of abuse compared to varnish and other standard finishes.

BMc: So like the earlier environments, the wood was left natural. But in the first two productions you used a dead white room. Now you began to use color on the walls and the ceiling. What effect did color have on the rest of the environment? What were you trying to get color to do?

RS: *Dionysus* was not dead white because most of the south wall was hung with thick red rugs and the north wall was built up with tiers for the audience. In *Commune* the walls and blue ceiling warmed the room, and created a sense of desert, but not a hostile desert. The ceiling blue spilled over the terra-cotta walls as if the sky were falling or like clouds. And there was a sense of humor in the room due to the graffiti. The audience scrawled all over the walls and over as much of the ceiling as they could reach. If the ceiling was the sky, then there was skywriting. There were slogans and drawings and messages on the ceiling and on the walls, scrawled in white, grey, red, and yellow chalk. Pictures were drawn and then rubbed out. The walls and ceiling were a kind of playground. This idea of graffiti came from the *Victims of Duty* environment which the New Orleans group did in 1967.

BMc: Graffiti was also used in the *Makbeth* maze. Chalk was left there for spectators to use as they cared to . What's the function of graffiti for the audience in these environments?

RS: There are various levels of participation. The most gross— I'm not using "gross" in a bad sense—is when the spectator becomes an actor. That happened in *Dionysus*. There was some

of it in *Commune*, but none of it in *Makbeth*. There are also more subtle forms of participation. Graffiti is a way of saying, "I was here." I like graffiti. I like it on the subways, I like it in the city, I think it's a popular art form—the people's version of murals. It's saying, "I exist as me, even in an environment that has left almost no room for individual statements." Graffiti has a spatial dimension, of course, but it also has a temporal dimension like the old blues moan: "I've been here and gone." But graffiti has an inverse temporal relationship, too. It lets you know that you'll extend into the future. Graffiti is like writing letters to someone you don't know but would like to meet. Graffiti actualizes what is usually denied in the orthodox theatre. In orthodox theatre, there is the illusion of an event taking place for the first time, or the last time, although we really know that it happened yesterday, and is going to happen tomorrow. Graffiti shows that this is neither the first nor last performance. The illusion of the first time doesn't add to the theatrical experience, it cheats you of the historicity, the temporal continuity, and ritualized sense of experience which is so comforting and so deeply a part of theatre.

BMc: One of the ghetto graffiti artists wrote that graffiti is very much like the experience of walking on a street in the ghetto and hearing a radio in every window. It's a kind of assertation of the reality of the lives of the ghetto inhabitants.

RS: It's an assertion of the reality of people who live in a temporal continuity and who have an oral culture. In an oral culture, you make your mark outside, in the environment.

BMc: What about costuming in *Commune*?

RS: *Commune* used character costuming. I said to the performers, "Suppose you're going out to the desert. You only have five dollars to spend. Here's $5, outfit yourselves." We were in New Paltz, about 60 miles from New York City. We went to Poughkeepsie one day and bought costumes. The premise was that we were going into Death Valley, so we needed things that were practical. And of course, things we liked. Joan came up with an apron; Spalding bought suspenders, which he wore over his regular dungarees; Steve Borst found white longjohns which he liked. Later on he got white overalls; Jim Griffiths found an army field jacket. The collection of stuff really did look like things people would wear in a commune because we went to the same stores that commune people went to. We embellished some. The budget went as high as $15 a person.

People got involved with different colors. Joan's costume was dominated by green and pinks. Jim's by grays; Spalding's by blue; Steve's by white, and so on. A very important costume element was introduced when we exchanged clothes with the audience or stole clothes from them. After the performance the things were returned, but occasionally a theft would be transformed into a gift and new costume elements entered the performance. There was an interesting flow of stuff—because performers would give or trade with the audience. The clothing was stolen in a scene about the robberies pulled off by the Manson family. Performers rushed among the audience and stole jewelry, coats, handbags, clothes, etc. Joan was particularly adept at exchanging clothes—she would find a woman and exchange her whole costume—dress, shirt, the whole thing. Nine out of ten times the person would exchange. Sometimes a handbag was stolen and its contents dumped out. "Look at what we got!", the thieves shouted and improvised with the stuff. Later during the scene showing the murder of Sharon Tate, performers took the audience's shoes—the audience members were forced to give up their shoes at the

beginning of the play— and wore them. Sometimes a few people rushed out to reclaim their shoes, not letting them be used in the play. In these ways spectators were implicated in the play. The costuming was cheap and effective. You want someone to really pay attention? Wear their coat—they'll watch you.

BMc: How did the use of light in *Commune* and *Makbeth* compare?

RS: *Commune* represented the first time that I consciously asked for general illumination with high spots. In *Dionysus* there were four or five light cues; in *Makbeth* there were many light cues. In *Dionysus* lighting involved mood; it was dim when spectators came in; it got rosy (the stage manager's gels) for the dance; it got very bright for birth and death. In *Commune* I wanted the room brightly lit, like a desert. But in this very bright area there were still brighter spots. We threw a lot of wide-open fresnels around, for general illumination and then we threw in ellipsoidals on different spots, and some very tightly focused fresnels on the same spots. The result was that places such as the Clementine circle, where the savages get killed in the southeast corner of the room, were very brightly lit. The tub was extremely brightly lit, and the reflection of the water played on the ceiling. The crest of the wave, as people came into and across the line marked "INSIDE" was very brightly lit. And several other places were very brightly lit. When a performer stepped into a circle of super-bright light within a whole room of bright light, it was like being outside on a day that is lightly clouded over, then, all of a sudden, the sun comes out. There was only one light cue. As the audience entered, the room was dim. There was a scene played in fairly dim light, and then there was a *High Noon* gunfight which ended with the words, "Bang! Bang! Bang!" On each "bang"

Commune model by Jerry Rojo. Photo: Barry Rimler

the lights were pushed up until everything was at full. The lights stayed there until after the audience left. I had to make sure the lights weren't turned off when the play was over. If the audience has been in theatre lights for a long time, it's a come-down to be dumped into house lights. Unless there's a reason for it, I like to have the audience go out in lights that they've become accustomed to. *Commune* ended with a question mark and a long silence. Then Spalding began to play his penny-whistle and Joan started to wash off her body paint in the tub. Others began to take off their costumes, put on their street clothes, and drift away. Sometimes the silence lasted three or four minutes, which is a long time. The whole coming down took another 10 or 15 minutes, while the audience re-claimed their shoes and drifted out.

During the My Lai sequence several important things were done in the center of the environment. For part of the run, 15 spectators were selected at random and asked to sit in a circle at the lowest dip of the wave, to represent the villagers of My Lai. Some of them stayed there for the rest of the play, forming an island of spectators in the middle of the wave. Beginning in April, 1971, we asked everyone in the room to sit on the wave. Usually everyone except for four or five people responded. The play began with maybe 100 people around the periphery, and three or four people in the center. Then with the My Lai sequence, which comes two-thirds of the way through, maybe 95 people crowded onto the wave, as though it were a boat in the center of emptiness, and four or five people on the outside, like combat photographers, crowded up against the walls. The performers were on the ramparts, too, saying Sergent Meadio's words about how the villagers of My Lai were murdered. Then after the My Lai sequence we said, "Now you can go back to where you were or maybe you want to change your

perspective." About 90 percent of them went back to the periphery, about half to the same place they came from, and the other half to new places. About ten people usually stayed in the center and watched the rest of the play from there.

The final version of the My Lai sequence: For the last couple of months of the run, we took the audience's shoes, put them on a large burlap blanket, dragged it up the wave and dumped the shoes into the center. They looked like the shoes of the concentration camps and of My Lai, the shoes of victims, and the shoes of wealth. This immense tangle of shoes stayed on the wave until the end of the play. When the play was over spectators came out to the middle to get their shoes. They met other spectators; they talked about the play. Some pulled their shoes out quickly, others more slowly, with sociability. That in itself made a very interesting spectacle as spectators sorted through a jungled pile of their property.

BMc: Can you describe the way you changed the *Commune* environment for *Concert for TPG?*

RS: *Concert for TPG* was a piece directed and composed by Paul Epstein. Paul arranged some of the music for *Dionysus*, composed the music for *Makbeth,* and composed and arranged music for *Commune.* After that, he composed *Concert,* which he directed. We took the wave apart and set up five of the sections as monoliths. They were free-standing, 8' to 10' high—like Stonehenge, with curved surfaces pointed towards the center and the framework exposed on the outside. The performers sometimes stood behind them and sometimes in front of them. Parts of their scores were hung behind. The audience either sat inside the circle or above it, or they could stand around it. Three feet in front of the curved face of each of the pieces—there were five performers, that's why we used five

Commune on tour. The play is just ending.

pieces of the wave—were music stands, which made a second circle. Then in dead center was a third circle of five sofa cushions of blue velvet. So we had four circles for the *Concert* environment: the circle of the pueblos, the second circle of the monoliths of the wave, the third circle of music stands, and the fourth circle of cushions. The action in the piece was highly formal. It was a musical piece without much narrative to it. The performers stood behind the Stonehenge pieces, in front of them, at the music stands, or they kneeled or sat on the cushions for the finale: a jam session combining body sounds and vocal sounds.

The wave was not designed to be used this way and the solution arose from a problem: "What should we do with the wave when we do *Concert,* which needs open space?" The wave had to be stored in the space—we came up with the idea of using it as part of an environment. The curved surfaces, incidentally, did some very nice things for the sound. The acoustics are good in the Garage, and curved wooden surfaces provided certain additional modulations. What started out as a problem became an asset.

BMc: What's been the relationship of finished environments to your expectations of those environments based on the models? Have you found things, or places, or possibilities, that you had not conceived of? Has the finished product moved you in different directions? I asked the question because it struck me, on the basis of the *Makbeth* environment, that when you came into a space for the first time, it seemed absolutely new to you. Not that you hadn't worked on the model, not that you hadn't seen the drawings, not that you hadn't been involved with the total concept, but the reality of the environment itself was totally new, pure potential, the beginning of another phase of an experiment.

RS: I have a very bad two-dimensional imagination. A drawing tells me nothing. I can't read elevations well. My eyes lose focus and I see double. I can't read for a long time at a stretch, or keep focus on one place. I suspect my handicap is one of the roots of my version of environmental theatre. I don't like movies. I go rarely and I usually fall asleep in the middle of TV programs. I like sports on TV because I've been to the spaces where they take place. I don't use my eyes that much in appraising a space. I use my ears and my hands. For a long time I didn't know that I don't see well in three dimensions, that I lack full stereoscopic vision. Unless I concentrate, I don't see in stereoscopic depth, I see blurred or double. I go into a space and sound it to get a full sense of it. When I look at the model it's the model I see. I can't easily extrapolate from the model to the space.

BMc: To what extent does the finished environment seem to act upon the work that you do?

RS: I never enter a space but that I'm amazed and astonished by it and that's what makes it fun to work in. When the model is realized in the space it's always a surprise to me. The model's like the space and not like it. So whenever anything is being built, it's very exciting for me, because then I begin to live in the space for the first time. Maybe other directors come into a space that is already familiar to them because they have approved the plans. But the way I work—the way my body works—no matter what the rendering is like, the model is new to me, and the actual space is new once again.

JR: Having worked in orthodox design quite a bit, I think there's another aspect. Part of the reason why you're amazed and astonished, is that you walk into a virgin space. In an orthodox theatre situation, the director has all of the information about a room that comes from its traditional associations. A kitchen has certain blocking patterns associated with it; living rooms are associated with different blocking patterns, and so on. But an environmental space has few of those associations. You have to create them organically out of the performers' and the director's inner feelings, a whole complex of relationships and events. It's virgin, new, and totally unique. That to me is the beautiful thing about this kind of work.

BMc: That's a very good point, because even non-representational stage settings seem to be a simplification and abstraction of an idea grounded in reality. You take the idea of an apartment building, for example, and abstract it and simplify it into a pipe framework. Here, in these environments, there is no attempt to work that way. The reference point is not a simplified castle for *Makbeth*. Rather what finally comes together out of experimentation on various aspects of the production is something like a castle.

RS: Yes. In orthodox theatre you work from the principle of abstraction. In environmental theatre you work from the principle of analogy. Analogic thought helps you construct something which may be like something else in functions, feel, or shape, but it is not taken from it—it has its own reality. Analogic thought may be as complicated as the thing of which it is an analogy, although it can be manipulated more easily, and is often reduced in size. Also a space lives its own life, projects its own logic. Finally, in a true environment, a full world is created, complex, contradictory, and dangerous.

COMMUNE

By The Performance Group and Richard Schechner
Music by The Performance Group from traditional
American sources
Musical consultant Paul Epstein
Assistant and then co-director Elizabeth LeCompte
Environment by Jerry N. Rojo
Directed by Richard Schechner
Opened December 17, 1970

Bruce White, then **Timothy Shelton** Bruce
Joan MacIntosh, then **Maxine Herman** Clementine
Stephen Borst David Angel
James Griffiths Fearless
*****Jayme Daniel** Jayson
Patricia Bower, then **Converse Gurian,** then
                Maxine Herman Lara/Lizzie
*****Mik Cribben** Mischa
Spalding Gray Spalding
*****Patric Epstein** Susan Belinda Moonshine

*In 2nd version of the play these roles were droppped.

13 The Tooth of Crime

The environment for Sam Shepard's *The Tooth of Crime* was designed by Jerry Rojo at the Frederic Wood Theatre at the University of British Columbia in Vancouver, where The Performance Group was in residence during the summer of 1972. The environment, which was designed to be easily broken down for storage or shipment, was later moved to the Performing Garage for the New York opening of *The Tooth of Crime*. The attempt was to develop a "starter" modular system for constructing environments, using Shepard's play as the basis for experimentation. The modules are made up of a system of ⅜" plywood panels which may be butted together in various ways. In the case of *The Tooth of Crime*, they were used to form a complex 30' long, 25' wide and 15' tall—a kind of cityscape with alleys, streets, rooms, window, doorways, and roofs. Both performers and audience members moved on, in, and about the complex during performance.

RS: *The Tooth of Crime* was begun in May, 1972. We worked on it a little bit in the empty Garage, with just a few fragments left from the *Commune* environment, which had been largely ripped down. Other plays had been done in there after *Commune*: The Manhattan Project's *Alice in Wonderland*, The Medicine Show Ensemble's piece, and a production of The Ridiculous Theatrical Company's *Eunuchs of the Forbidden City*. We worked in the Garage for a month or so, and then we worked in a room at Berkeley. Then we went to the University of British Columbia in Vancouver, and we worked in a large 40' by 40' by 10' room. Finally, we worked on the main stage of the Frederic Wood Theatre. While we agreed to perform on this modern proscenium stage, we knew that we would invite the audience onto the stage either with the front curtain up or with it closed. We treated that space as if it were the Garage.   Jerry was able to spend a consecutive number of weeks with us.

BMc: Would you explain the modules? What was the principles behind them?

JR: The modular system is a system of two-dimensional units. The simpler the component, it seems to me, the better the modular system. But that simple component should be able to be expanded into a very complex environment if necessary. The charge here was to create a modular system, without any very direct connection to *The Tooth of Crime*. Obviously, by watching rehearsals and knowing the Group itself, I was conscious of *Tooth*. But my attempt was to find a basic system, and we really explored a lot of possibilities.

BMc: Can you explain some of those possibilities?

JR: We needed to have, as I said, the simplest component, in this case a two-dimensional unit that could be stored. The unit had to come out of Vancouver and go to New York City, which is 3,000 miles away. It also had to tour; plus there was the possibility of its being used for other completely unrelated environments. It was a modular system that would be put together, taken apart, and put together again countless times. We started with the idea of a two-dimensional module—in this case a sheet of plywood. What could you do with that piece of plywood? One thing would be to take it down to its lightest possible weight and yet develop a high-rise ability. High-rise was important. Of course, above a certain size, weight becomes a problem, so it was a matter of finding the right formula. The formula, I suppose, grew out of boat construction. A boat has to be light but strong because the dynamics of water and sail call for a very,very delicate kind of weight/size ratio. So we worked it out. We worked with the technical director of UBC, Norman Young, who was very knowledgeable, very helpful, very interested in coming to grips with the problem. We took our ideas to him: he knew the town of Vancouver, and he could take us to people who were working in aluminum and plywood. He led us to all the right sources. We decided on ⅜" plywood as the lightest possible weight; beyond that the units would be too flexible.

BMc: Would you describe the modular system?

JR: The system was a series of ⅜" plywood panels with holes cut into them. The holes were there both to reduce weight and also for visual reasons.

BMc: Give me an example of how a panel might be made.

JR: Well, let's say a panel was 3' wide. Because we worked on 1' intervals it would therefore have a 1' wide hole cut in it, 6' high if the panel were, let's say 8'. There were also small holes drilled in 2" and 8" centers, so that any panel could be butted on to any other panel in any perpendicular configuration.

BMc: If you were butting two units together, what would you use to join them?

JR: We used aluminum angle brackets, 3" square, on a side. To accommodate any kind of butting each bracket had one hole on one angle and four holes on the other. For more than a hundred panels we used close to a thousand brackets. The modular system was to be a starter group. Instead of building a system of arbitrary units, we designed a module to fit *Tooth*. We could then add curves, or diagonals, or platforms, and so on.

BMc: These units, then, can be knocked down and stored flat. Can they be shipped relatively easily?

RS: They're self-packing. When we shipped them from Vancouver to New York, the two outermost panels became the

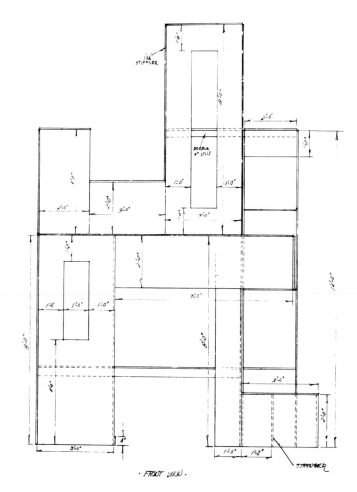

Working drawing of vertical section for *The Tooth of Crime* modular system by Jerry Rojo.

shipping "crate." We just wrapped them in steel bands. If the outside got banged up, we just made two more.

BMc: Did you adapt this modular system to the demands of *Tooth?*

RS: Since the theory is that you can build anything out of the modules, we decided to make a model of *Tooth* and then build it out of the modules. The modules were tailormade for *The Tooth of Crime* but we hoped we could do other things with them. And knowing that, we may well use them again. Some of them are being used in *Mother Courage,* but in a cannabilized way.

BMc: Aside from portability and ease of storage, what did you want out of these modules—especially in terms of *Tooth?*

RS: The idea of the *Tooth* modules was that there would be three towerlike units that looked like telephone booths mounted on a central structure. I wanted something to dominate the center of the room. Everytime I've directed I got back to a kind of arena, whether it was the table in *Makbeth,* or the wave in *Commune,* or the black mats in *Dionysus.* So I said to myself that the problem this time would be to put something in the center and see what happens in terms of the staging; if something were in the center, it would make it impossible to do arena staging.

JR: That's exactly what we did. We created these units—these stacked telephone booths if you want to call them that—but, originally, they were in two different parts of the room. Then we brought them together.

BMc: Will you describe the location and appearance of those units in the Garage?

JR: First of all, the plywood flat unit was roughly 30' long and 20' wide, and 15' tall, at the highest point. There were two major towers connected by a bridge. Then there was an outrigger that grew off one of the towers, and a right angle avenue off of that. The unit was filled with simulated wombs, compartments, companionways, and steel ladders that allowed audience and performer to get up to the different spaces. It was a kind of microcosm of a cityscape. The floor was painted black so the unit sat in a sea of blackness. The plywood was sealed with polyurethane, which has an amber quality, but the plywood grain showed through. And of course, there were holes in each unit, and the bolts and the hardware all were visible.

BMc: What was the color of the walls in the Garage for this production?

JR: White, with a blue ceiling. Another, interesting point is that while this unit was the primary performance unit in the Garage, we also installed a ring around the room which establishes a "permanent" gallery. The gallery was constructed out of material from earlier environments. While it is of wood, it hasn't at all the same feeling as the center unit, which resembled a giant modular toy system much like a house of cards.

RS: The gallery has two levels. On part of the south wall and all of the west wall it's about 7 ½" high, and along the northeast wall it's 11'. This is very important for *Tooth* because near the lower gallery on the floor is the bed. The result is an intimate space, while the upper gallery surrounds a public space. The unit in the center of the room really doesn't ever have much audience on it. Even on a very crowded night there may only be 15 or 20 people up there. Most of the center unit of *Tooth* is only 3' or 4' wide, and in using it the performers chase most

spectators from it. Most of the audience is in the galleries on the floor. We painted the floor shiny black because it suggested a street to me, and a TV sound stage. The few spectators who are on the central structure are really in the middle of the play, much more so than in our other shows.

BMc: Another difference from the other productions is that the audience moves through the center unit frequently. The audience passes through the center at floor level at the same time that the performers are working above them or next to them, only a few inches away. Much of *Tooth*, in fact, is really a kind of street theatre, with a continuous flow of audience. It's like an audience at a street fair or a carnival, with a much stronger senses of movement than in any of the earlier pieces.

JR: If you watched an accident on the street, for example, you might climb a telephone pole to see it, because of other people in front of you. Here the audience made choices about how to see the production because the environment provided places for them to crawl up on and to frame off scenes.

RS: I'm very happy with *Tooth* in terms of space. There are differences between those scenes where the audience is on the same level as the performers, and the other scenes where performers are on the central structure and the spectators gather on the floor and crane their necks to look up.

BMc: The same thing is true of the burlesque scene where people are constantly craning to look up at the platform where Joan does her tassle dance.

BMc: What about costumes in *The Tooth of Crime?*

RS: The *Tooth of Crime* was the most orthodox of my productions at the Garage. I had just come back from Asia in April, 1972, I wanted to re-establish myself in the group. When I

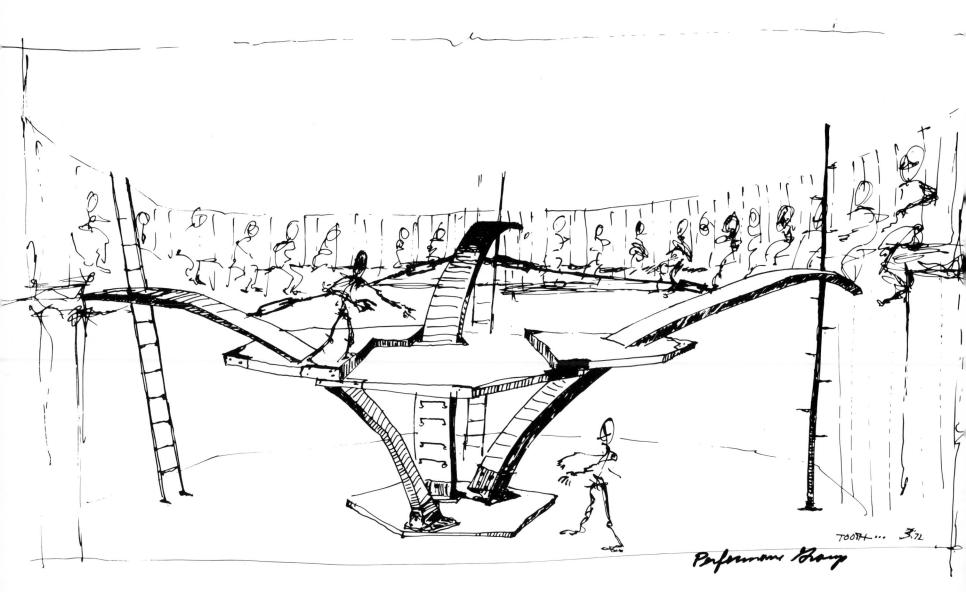

TOOTH... 太72

Performance Group

Preliminary study for *The Tooth of Crime*, not used in final project. Rendering by Jerry Rojo.

The Tooth of Crime. Cheyenne talks to Hoss at the end of Act I. They are sitting at the breakfast table in the southeast corner of the environment.

The Tooth of Crime, Act I. Cheyenne talks to Hoss as seen through a window in the module.

had problems with the first Group at the end of *Makbeth*, I booted people out. In the second Group, when there were problems, they cut me down to size. I didn't play my full deck of cards in *The Tooth of Crime*. Maybe that was lucky. First of all, I accepted somebody else's play. Shepard's play wasn't forced on me—I loved it—but I was doing things carefully. After working on the play for about six months, we hired a costume designer, Franne Lee. Franne used the same principles anybody uses in orthodox productions: She read the play. She watched rehearsals, she came up with ideas. The performers added to the costumes, personalized them. Franne picked up most of the costumes in second-hand shops; I liked that. It gave a nice, almost worn-out feel to them—run down wealth. There is more than a little Tennessee Williams in Shepard. The costumes were too funky to show a wealthy rock world, and too costumey to be real funk. It wasn't Franne's fault. I never settled on exactly what I wanted. Also, before hiring Franne, we worked with a costumer during the summer at 1972 at the University of British Columbia. He and I just didn't see eye to eye. Then Franne had to go on to other jobs, so really we only worked together for two or three months, and that's not long enough. *Tooth* never came together totally in terms of costumes.

As usual, some of the critics were recalcitrant. Clive Barnes sat on the edge of the southeast gallery, which is one of the few places from which you can see everything—but much of it from a great distance. Stanley Kauffman sat on the stairway in the northwest corner, and didn't see half the play. Marilyn Stasio, who liked the production a lot, picked the one place on the center unit where she could stay in one location and see everything clearly. But she was still in one place. Critics seem to have an occupational distaste for anything but the orthodox situation. They fix themselves in the space and then complain about the staging. In *Tooth* where the root metaphor is movement, it's really bizarre to have somebody say, "I couldn't see or hear." It's like going to a cafeteria and saying you weren't waited on—complaining you couldn't get anything but soup because you stood in front of the soup tureen all night.

BMc: In popular forms nobody seems to have this problem. For example, in a carnival midway, or in an amusement park, the audience is mobile simply because the entertainment is designed for a mobile audience. Does the different placement of the central unit in this environment imply a different kind of lighting?

JR: Richard mentioned lights were built into the central units themselves, like a big electric doll's house. Also the concept of television or film studio lighting. For scenes that had very high intense lighting, like a prizefight, we used parabolic floodlights with concentrated parallel rays. The result was pockets of light.

BMc: So the light was coming from a number of different directions, into and out of the central unit.

RS: Yes. And some of the lights were very close in, much closer than in anything else we've done. Some were only two or three feet away from the performers. The parabolic reflection over the bed was very close in—like over an operating table. When performers stood on the bed, there was less than six inches between them and the light.

JR: The rigging for lights inside the central unit was important because it added a whole new scenic element. The cable and the pipes and the lights and all of that paraphernalia suggested telephone poles and street lights—things you associate with city lights. The audience looked through all of this and I think it became a visually important part of the environment.

We were thinking about taking these modules up to Connecticut and turning them over to the design students. We'll put them in a room 25' square and have the design students work with them to try to develop a sense of rhythm and a sense of what works spatially, using a full-scale model. Even if students are interested in box sets or some other kind of traditional design, I think the modules can be used as an effective teaching tool.

BMc: That sounds very good for scene design students who usually work only with designs or small models, and have no sense of the reality of full space. By the time they work in real space the use of the space is fixed. That's bad. Your plan will introduce playing into design. These modules will allow them to deal with the reality of surface and shapes as they actually would be in performance instead of distancing themselves through drawings and models.

THE TOOTH OF CRIME

By Sam Shepard
Music by The Performance Group
Costumes by Franne Lee
Environment by Jerry N. Rojo
Directed by Richard Schechner
Opened March 7, 1973

*Stephen Borst Galactic Max, Doc
 Spalding Gray Hoss
 James Griffiths Cheyenne
 Elizabeth LeCompte Star, Ref
 Joan MacIntosh Becky Lou
 Timothy Shelton Crow

*Later this role was rotated with Leeny Sack.

14 Mother Courage and Her Children

James Clayburgh,
co-designer of *Mother
Courage*, joined the
authors in this discussion.

Mother Courage, developed by The Performance Group, opened at The Performing Garage in February of 1975. The idea to perform *Mother Courage* arose while the Group was working on *The Marilyn Project*. They were looking for a play that had good roles for women, one that they would enjoy working on, and one that had a political core. The Group accepted the Manheim translation of the script, except for the songs—which Richard Fire, Mercedes Gregory, and Richard Schechner retranslated—and turned to scenic exploration. The space was co-designed by Jerry Rojo and Jim Clayburgh. Clayburgh has designed with the Group, Michael McClure's *The Beard*, directed by Stephen Borst, *Sakonnet Point* by Spalding Gray and Elizabeth LeCompte, and *Claiming The Body*, a collective piece from a workshop that Borst directs.

BMc: Do you consider it unusual for TPG to do a classical author like Brecht?

RS: No, we did Euripides and Shakespeare. It is unusual for us to do a play we can't take apart and put back together. But that was the case with *Tooth*, too. What I loved about *The Tooth of Crime* was its language. The language of *Courage* in English isn't as rich as it is in German. But we accepted the script as translated. I didn't know what I wanted to do—but whatever, it was to be without a wagon. Although there was a phase in the summer of 1974 when we rehearsed using a costume trunk as a rolling unit.

JR: One idea was an elaborate soap box derby unit with the whole lighting board on the wagon—every element of the show coming out of the wagon—but that was very early.

RS: This is the only project of The Performance Group which we worked on from beginning to end only in the Garage. We designed *Courage* as we were building it—action design—rather than conceptualizing it, then building it.

JR: With this project Jim Clayburgh took on the real implementation of the space. He was always on the job. During July-August, 1974, all three of us worked to firm up the idea. But then—to make the performers part of the mechanics of the space—Clayburgh worked out the details of the block and tackle system.

BMc: If you were designing as you were building—what were the parameters?

JR: One of the early things was the modular scaffolding system which was partially paid for by a National Endowment for the Arts grant of $3,750.

JC: Actually the scaffolding came before *Mother Courage*. It was part of *The Marilyn Project*.

BMc: What were you looking for in the scaffolding?

JR: Since *Tooth* we have been working with the idea of a modular system—to find a very flexible scaffolding system that can develop shapes that are rectilinear, polygonal and other odd shapes. Initially, I thought that *Courage's* wagon might be the scaffolding. Not that it would move—but possibly the performers could put the wagon together during the show. In that way all of the scenes would grow out of this basic structure which was a microcosm of Mother Courage's home industry. Richard rejected that because he didn't want the center of the space occupied.

RS: We had just done a center space environment with *Tooth*. I didn't want to repeat it. There was something when we began working on *Courage* that was so rich, so epic, so long, that I had to make the basic choice of whether to shorten it or

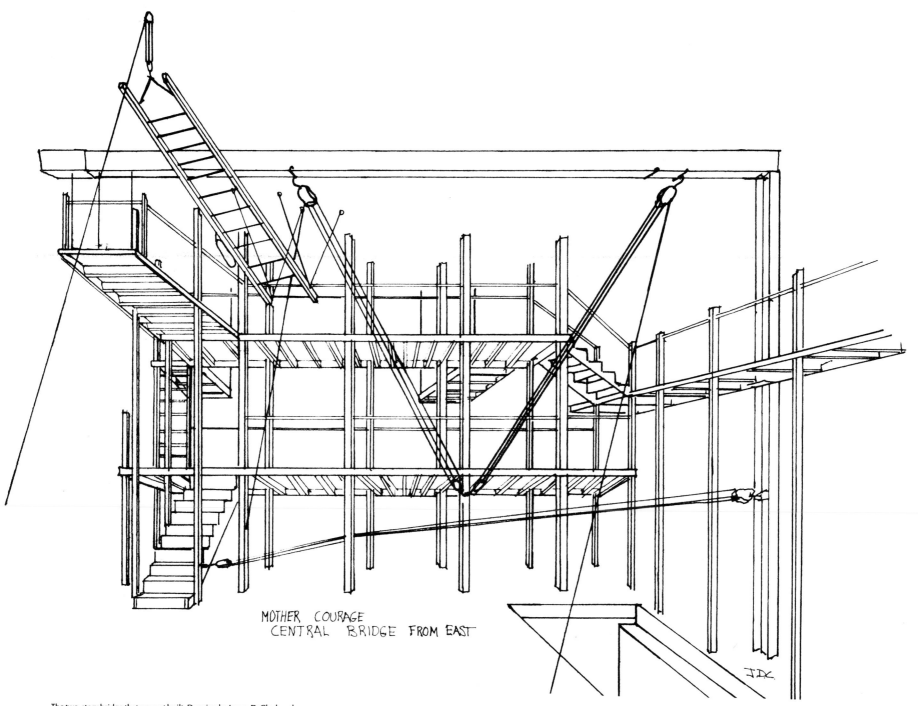

MOTHER COURAGE
CENTRAL BRIDGE FROM EAST

The two-story bridge that was not built. Drawing by James D. Clayburgh.

Preliminary study of Mother Courage's wagon using aluminum module system. Drawing by Jerry Rojo.

let it take its own time—an epic in the tradition of *Gone With the Wind*. Adding supper for the audience made it even longer, nearly four hours. To do this I needed lots of open space that could change into many different spaces. Finally the ropes were the answer. No one knew this at first.

BMc: How did the idea of the ropes and pulleys develop?

RS: We began work upstairs because we were still performing *The Tooth of Crime* downstairs. We worked on the first scene and pulled a trunk across the floor, but everytime we pulled something that rolled, we inevitably got thrown back on the Berliner Ensemble production. That was repugnant to me. If I had to stick to the text I didn't want to stick to the staging. It would take away our own possibilities for exploration. So we gave up the idea of a wagon—though not the idea of pulling and physical labor. Then came the wheel—how can we do pulling and labor without a wagon?

JC: The wheel came out of watching rehearsals upstairs and realizing that it wasn't necessary to move a wagon. The thought of a treadmill was eliminated quickly because it is very close to the Berliner Ensemble's revolve.

RS: We were aiming at something which took real work.

JC: And the wheel was an extension of that.

BMc: Would you please describe the wheel?

JC: It was going to be 8' in diameter, set into the garage floor pit about 2' down and rising about 6' up from the floor level. Constructed from angle irons and wood.

JR: So that it would be like a ferris wheel or a laboratory rat wheel-trap.

JC: It was big enough so that two people could run inside it showing the physical work but not getting anywhere. The outside was to be used like a torture wheel for Swiss Cheese's and Eilif's deaths.

RS: And also the wheel gave the idea that the whole Garage was a wagon and that this was just one of four wheels moving the Garage.

JR: Also, it localized the war machine itself. Out of the war-machine image came the idea of leverage which led to the block and tackle. We were talking about a wheel that people could run in. We were also talking about putting motors on it—putting gear ratios on it to have it at a lot of different speeds and have the performers actually move the wheel.

BMc: Why did the wheel get rejected?

RS: It was a theatrical abstraction—brilliant but a metaphor rather than an actuality. *Mother Courage* is a very "unsatisfactory play" and at the end, people should say, "I like the person Mother Courage but I don't like her, too. I understand why she did what she did. It was a good experience but it wasn't so good." The wheel was too satisfying and fulfilling. Also the wheel would weight the space. It would draw attention to itself even when not in use. It would be the focus of movement within the space. At about the time we were discussing the idea of using the street in front of the theatre. Actually, for *The Marilyn Project* we were going to build a little proscenium inside the garage and the audience would go outside the Garage and watch from Wooster Street.

BMc: That's an idea you've been talking about for a long time. The proscenium would face the street through what is the garage door?

Eilif and Swiss Cheese pull the wagon in *Mother Courage*, Scene 1. Photo: Clem Fiori

RS: Yes, the proscenium would have been set in the garage door facing into the street. The audience would go out in the street and look back into the theatre at a little proscenium. But using the street contradicted using the wheel. If we used the street and the wheel was one of the four wheels of the Garage, there was no reason to go outside. So here was this huge brilliant metaphor that could only be used three or four times. It contradicts the play's basic action which is: Everything is practical, is turned to labor.

JC: The wheel goes against Brecht. He would deplore an abstraction like that. It is a rich man's device. The way the space is now—the performers change it themselves. The common man's thing is directly working in the space.

JR: We came close to building that wheel. We had the money. We had the drawings. We were all here ready to go. Then one day there was a rehearsal with pulleys and ropes. It was that night the wheel was rejected.

JC: It came out of a workshop where each performer went into a harness and one person would hold the lead rope, having leverage, and a struggle between master and slave went on. The physical images were so strong. For example, Steve Borst leaned over the pit knowing he would fall if the other person let the rope slip.

RS: That's an image still used in Scene 7.

BMc: When you started using the block and tackle in the workshop, how much of the space was occupied with what is now the environment?

JC: The Wooster Street side and the north wall.

RS: The pier jutting out from the north wall used to be a bridge cutting the space into two: a large one on the Wooster Street side and a smaller one to the west. Actually the bridge was made by flip-flopping part of the low gallery of *Tooth*. We kept the bridge through open rehearsals in December, 1974. One night we had 100 people in here and many of them couldn't see. The next afternoon we changed the bridge to a pier.

BMc: You cut it off?

RS: About 10' and moved it over to the south wall.

JC: And added a second platform high on the south wall. But before striking the bridge we almost did the opposite—built a second story onto it so that more people could sit over the middle of the space. But sight lines would have been bad from the rest of the room, and we wanted to play to audiences of at least 150. With the bridge one or two stories, the audience would be limited to under 100.

RS: Part of the decision was the result of asking the audience what they liked. Certain things I listen to from the audience—other things, no. What is the difference? Well, if the audience says "this is too long—I can't really stay here for the whole thing," that doesn't make me cut it but find find ways of bringing in variety. But if they can't see, and I know they should see, then the environment or staging must be changed. And the reaction of the audience—of people who saw the space with the bridge and without it—was unanimous: it is better without it. Spectators don't give a damn about "environmental design"—they give a damn about seeing the play.

JR: This way of working includes real negotiations. That's what I like about it.

BMc: In discussions of other projects you said it didn't matter that much about whether people could see. You said that you

The audience eats supper between
Scenes 3 and 4. Photo: Clem Fiori

liked the idea of having them move. Is the audience confined to one spot?

RS: The audience moves three times, and each move is related to the basic movements of the play. The play is in four basic movements—the first movement is the "theatrical" movement from the beginning to supper (Scenes One through Three). Supper is the second movement and it brings almost everyone down on the floor. It looks like a picnic on the battlefield.

JR: And like a Depression kitchen line.

RS: They literally wait and get soup ladled out to them. Scene Four is a song sung cabaret-style at the end of supper. Supper is a "social" event. Scenes Five through Eight are a second "theatrical" movement. It is usually more relaxed and more intense than the first movement. More people are sitting on the floor. They are friendly and full of food. The people who didn't like the production leave during supper—the break lasts about 35 minutes. So everyone who remains really supports the performance—and we all feel it adds an intensity, a ritual element. The fourth movement is "actual." The Garage door opens—the weather and energies of the street barge into the theatre. Many people are on the floor for Scenes Nine through Twelve. For the final scene, 40 or 50 people stand around in their coats which makes it look like a street scene. The final scene shows Courage stripping Kattrin down to her underwear. In this scene when Kattrin is being dragged to the pit, sometimes spectators walk over to look at that. Outside in the street people walk by, police cars cruise—spectators laugh at ironies. The contrast between the reality of the theatre and that of the street is brutal and funny.

RS: The original idea was to have three spaces. A private space near the west wall, a big space opposite the open pit, and a green room that the audience could see into in the northwest corner. Costume changes took place in the green room, and performers relaxed there. The life of the theatre and the life of the wagon are contrasted. For example, when Courage leaves the space while Swiss Cheese runs away with the cash box, she is seen resting or reading a magazine. Actually what happened during the run was that two green rooms emerged—the one the audience would see and another back in the technical area behind the visible green room. Performers went to the truly off-stage space to talk, smoke, and get away. I don't know if it's possible in our culture (or anywhere) to have a performance with absolutely no backstage.

BMc: What were you doing, Jerry?

JR: I was in three days a week for two months during the summer. Each time a new problem came up and we would work on the solution.

JC: Each rope came into being to solve concrete problems. For example, hanging and killing Swiss Cheese, giving Yvette a tent, dividing the space into Courage's tent and the rainy outside in Scene Six.

JR: The attempt was to find a physicalization in ropes for each scene. In Scenes 1, 7, 8, 9, 10, and 12, ropes were used mechanically to pull; in Scenes 2, 3, 5, and 6 they divided the space. In some scenes they were used both ways. For example in Scene 3, the space is changed twice by moving the rope, and the ropes are used to hang Swiss Cheese over the large playing area. At the end of the Scene, after he is shot, his corpse is lowered to the floor and then dragged into the pit. The ropes were constantly used both as space markers and as active

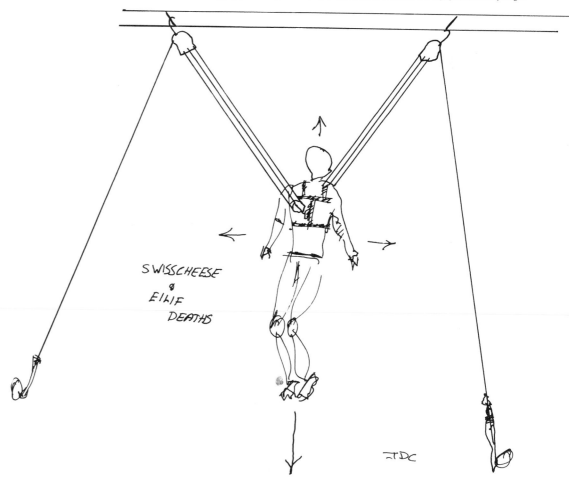

SWISSCHEESE
&
EILIF
DEATHS

JDC

instruments of work and war. There were anchor points on the walls, ceiling and floor for the ropes. And above the bridge was a wire guideline at 14' so that we could shift the ropes across the space easily. The scene shifts themselves—done in full light—involved the whole company and the restructuring of the ropes. The shifts were very important—they were the actual work of building a theatre space and transforming it. The scenes of murder and execution are literally played off the floor—each of Courage's children is killed in mid-air. When the person is dropped or falls, the pain of the sudden stop at the end of the rope is a cruel experience analagous to being executed.

RS: This particular space developed in jumps rather than along a smooth evolutionary curve. It was almost an ideal situation for environmental theatre—three people who know each other very well working with a group that has been stable for five years. We have many years working together in a space that we know. Instead of working through drawings, models, constructions and so on, a lot of things happened in bursts. Two important structures were built in bursts—the complicated polygonal "wagon-store" and adjacent structures against the west wall and the supermarket posters combined with the Marine Corps enlistment posters on the south wall. Other spatial decisions—like the division of the theatre into three basic spaces also happened impulsively.

BMc: How long did it all take?

RS: The first thing was the establishment of the three spaces as soon as The Tooth of Crime finished at the end of June, 1974. The construction of the wagon-store complex occurred in two bursts, one in July when Jerry, Jim, and Bruce Rayvid constructed it on a Saturday morning. The beauty of this alumi-

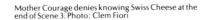

num scaffolding is that it is very light, flexible, easy to construct and to deconstruct. Then the second burst happened in December when the bridge was taken down and the high gallery was built along the south wall—making the room into a complete arena.

JC: We thought about doing the whole garage in advertising and enlistment posters—the ceiling, walls, the floor, the inside of the pit.

BMc: And it ends up being on half of one wall.

RS: When we put it up one Saturday morning in December, it was such a startling effect. We felt one-half a wall was enough. Before, in July, we knew the Depression was coming. We geared this whole thing to Depression.

JR: It becomes less a war play and more a play about economics.

RS: How do you make a living in tough times? We emphasize money in our posters, everywhere, even in our prices (you know $1.99, $2.89, $3.98, $4.95), and a soup-line supper for $1.99.

JR: Everything is functional—the bursts come when the performers need something, then you build it.

RS: In July or August, we decided to serve supper as part of the play, so in Scene 3 we actually had to set up supper. Serving tables are set in the southwest corner; a rope is put up to control people's access to the food, a cash register is set up near the pit, so right after Swiss Cheese is dumped into the pit, Jim Clayburgh comes out and says, "The end of Part One—supper will now be served."

BMc: What are you serving?

RS: Soup, cheese, bread, butter, beverage, fruit for $1.99.

BMc: The materials that are in the space—how did they come about?

JR: The space is totally cannibalized—wood from *Dionysus*, things off the street, ladders from *Tooth*.

BMc: Could we be more specific?

JR: Only the aluminum scaffolding which is the wagon-store complex, the gallery on the south wall, and the ropes and pulleys were designed specifically for this production. The surrounding galleries and the pier were from *Tooth*. The advertising stuff was all collected, the floor was painted by Herbert Blau's group when they used the space in August, 1974.

RS: The black floor of *Tooth* shows through at some points and the raw wood of *Commune* shows, too.

BMc: And the ceiling is blue.

RS: Left over from *Commune*. The decks of some platforms are from the modules of *Tooth*. It gives the feeling of war surplus. We didn't try to cover up past productions. I believe in collage, and in Group history.

BMc: Let's talk about the scaffolding.

JR: It is in 4′ × 6′ units—some are ladder-type units—others make an arch, others are simply tubes.

BMc: Did you buy them in those unit shapes?

JR: No, I designed it and had it built by a welding company. The individual parts are connected to each other by pins, which fit to the ends of these 4′ × 6′ units. So we can really create any

kind of shape. They work like door hinges which pivot. Also there are bleacher units. We can keep adding more and more.

RS: It is very good for touring, light, flexible, easily trucked.

BMc: And the ropes?

RS: Essentially ship's rigging. The ropes transform the space. In Scene One there is a rope cutting the space from north to south—a roadblock. Courage and her children are on one side and the Sargeant and the Recruiter are on the other side. The scene is about the military people stealing Eilif by getting him across the ropes. In Scene Two, a rope cuts diagonally across the southeast corner which becomes the kitchen. Simultaneously in the northwest over the green room, are the General, the Chaplain, and Eilif. In Scene Three, there is a complicated web of ropes that divides the space into Yvette's tent, Courage's store, and the battlefield. Several times during the scene, the ropes are changed: during the battle Courage's area shrinks, after Swiss Cheese is arrested he is hauled into the air; then Courage sets up her supper by hauling a rope from north to south. Courage is in the southwest, isolated behind the rope she put up, bargaining to save Swiss Cheese. When Swiss Cheese is killed, Courage ducks under the rope, examines his corpse, and denies she knows him. He's dragged off, hauled over the pit, and dropped in. Jim Clayburgh worked out the details of how to handle and manipulate the ropes. *Courage* is not an empty center arena setting because the center is full of ropes. Ropes and light towers dropped from the grid to within 7′ of the floor make the center space into many slices, cubes, and polygons of three-dimensional space.

JC: Each particular rope was originated for a particular use in staging. But all the ropes serve multiple functions—to haul people, to hold them, and to define the space.

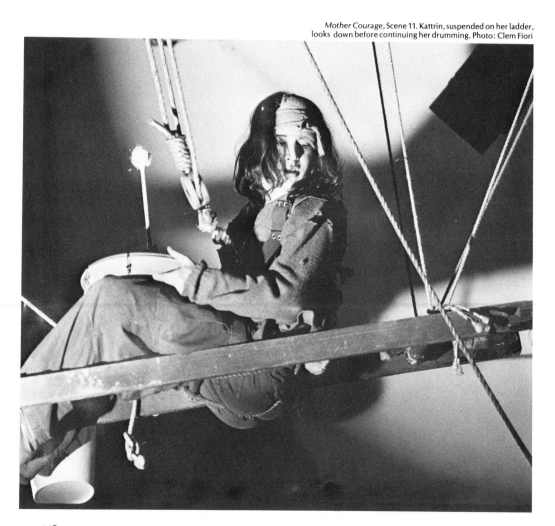

Mother Courage, Scene 11. Kattrin, suspended on her ladder, looks down before continuing her drumming. Photo: Clem Fiori

BMc: What about Kattrin's death?

RS: Well, it's spectacular. She's shot and she falls off a ladder into mid-air, about 12′ off the floor. She climbs the ladder and then pulls it up until it is horizontal—and really no one can reach her up there. When she gets up there she attaches herself to a safety rope. She is up there, drumming, and she is shot—she falls 1½′ before the rope catches her, and then she dangles in the space. During the scene change between Eleven and Twelve, Clayburgh lowers the safety rope bringing Kattrin back to the floor.

BMc: Is she wearing a harness?

RS: Yes. All the deaths are in harness. People are animals, they work and die in harness. Also the food comes down from our kitchen on the second floor of the building and the dirty dishes go back up through a ceiling trap. The food is hauled on ropes and pulleys.

BMc: It's the same trap used for *Makbeth*?

JR: Yes. Actually a trap within a trap. The *Makbeth* trap was a 4′ × 8′ trap and in it we cut a little 2′ × 2′ trap.

RS: It was part of the original building.

BMc: How about the scenes played in Wooster Street?

RS: At the end of Scene Eight, war starts again; Courage is happy (peace depresses her). She, the Cook, and Kattrin march right through the overhead Garage door as it opens—they march into Wooster Street. The rope extends from the back of the Garage right into the middle of the street. The audience sees the Garage being extended into the street.

JR: The ropes, the harnesses, the costumes, the street scenes,

Mother Courage, Scene 9. Courage and the Cook sing for their breakfast on cold Wooster Street as the audience watches. Photo: Clem Fiori

149

The company sings and marches the first song. Photo: Clem Fiori

give a beautiful image of the play. During the last few scenes, the audience, bundled in coats, comes onto the open floor to sit or stand watching the play as if it were a street play. It all is unified at the end, after nearly four hours.

BMc: Did you do a lot of research on block and tackles, pulleys, and harnesses?

JC: The block and tackles were all specially arranged by us, from standard stuff which we got on Canal Street—one of the last great junk and hardware marketing districts. The harnesses are our own invention. They have no function outside of *Mother Courage*. Swiss Cheese, who is suspended for over 25 minutes, is in a parachute harness because it became terribly uncomfortable for him to be suspended for 25 minutes in one of our harnesses.

RS: At the end of the play, Courage strips Kattrin to her underwear. She gathers all of Kattrin's clothes, her drum, and her harness. Courage looks like one of those "I live out of a shopping bag" street women of New York. She gathers up every rope in the room. There is a web of ropes in which she is enmeshed, still marching. For about 30 performances the play ended with her immobilized in her own web. Now she marches off toward the pit. It is less pretty, more truthful. The last image is of her black military boots marching, her head bent, the red boots offered for sale to the corpses singing in the pit.

BMc: The harnesses became the costumes. What other costumes are there?

RS: Theodora Skipitaris designed the costumes. Actually she collected most of them. We wanted costumes from second-hand stores, from Army surplus. The colors were chosen carefully; purple for Yvette, olive drab for enlisted men, pastels for Courage becoming more tattered as the time passes. The only really bright color is for the red boots—they blaze.

BMc: Is there a particular period?

RS: No. Different scenes were anachronistic in different ways. In Scenes Three and Eight, Courage wears rollers in her hair—a surburban American housewife. Kattrin wore drab colors and bulky clothes. The soldiers were in olive with caps, helmets, boots; the knives and ax were real, and dangerous. Nine performers played more than twenty roles. The costumes established classes of characters: soldiers, farmers, workers, officers, and so on. In Scene Two, Elizabeth LeCompte plays the General. She wears a carefully built mustache made from her own hair, and a World War One officer's jacket. Swiss Cheese, who is the dutiful son, wears a boy scout uniform with long underwear underneath. Eilif, the hero-braggart son, wears a Green Beret jump suit. In Scenes Five, Six and Seven, Courage wears a Red Cross uniform. At the end of the play she is dressed like a New York street woman. A lot of the costumes the performers designed themselves by picking out different things.

JR: Brecht talks about "the historification of events," bringing all forms to the center rather than being unified in one period. We bring different points of history to one place, different experiences of war. War makes people into scavengers.

BMc: Are you happy with the costumes?

RS: Yes, but what I would really like is a new member of the Group to become our permanent costumer.

JR: The performer in this kind of work has a great input into what they are going to wear. They are much more conscious of what the costume looks like than what the scaffolding looks like. This can be a problem because if the director wants this look and the performer wants it to look that way and the costumer wants it to look another way—then it gets sticky.

RS: In our Group the performer has the final word because I've found that gives some very idiosyncrantic costumes which I like very much.

JR: Except for *Makbeth* which was standardized.

RS: The hatreds in the Group during that production made it necessary to standardize.

BMc: Let's move on to the lighting.

JC: The only general conceptual element was that we wanted the scene shifts to be in the brightest possible light.

RS: People need to see clearly when they are working. We emphasize work, and the work of the production is "how to tell the story." It is not a story about work but work about telling a story about work, business, war.

JC: We drop two towers into the space again, as we did with *Tooth*.

RS: I love to force the audience to look through the equipment. It exercises their attention—they have to work a little to see.

JC: It makes people more aware that they are in a theatre. The physical presence of the lights should be designed as consciously as the light which is projected by it.

JR: The orthodox approach to lighting is that you light from

outside to inside. Here we light from inside to outside. I took that idea to its logical extreme in Shaliko's *Ghosts* where all lighting was practical.

BMc: The lighting that's not on the trees—where is it?

JC: On three pipes—one in the center and two pipes to the north and south of it.

JR: And there are some practicals in the wagon, and under the galleries. Scene Six is lit mostly by practicals.

BMc: What happens to the light when the audience goes outside?

RS: The audience stays inside and looks through the Garage door as if it were a proscenium.

JC: The performers are lit by two small reflecting spotlights aimed up at them from knee level. These lights are mounted inside the theatre, close to the door. They function like sharp footlights. The theatre is kept lit just enough for the performers to see the audience. Generally, the lights in the theatre are kept bright enough so that the performers can see the audience and to get reaction and feedback from them. Many lines are delivered directly to spectators. In this way the play's story is told, its feelings are shared, its questions asked.

BMc: What about the pit?

RS: About 15' of it is open, which is less than half of it. The pit is always there—the mass grave, the garbage dump, the open wound in the space.

BMc: And some of the other peripheral areas?

RS: Ron Vawter, our general manager actually sits under the pier on the south side doing the business of the Group, counting the night's receipts in full public view, writing letters, typing. He also plays drums and two small roles. Everywhere we showed the process of our working. Jim Clayburgh plays small roles too. From November 1975, after Tim Shelton left the group, Clayburgh played Eilif. We wanted to erase some of the divisions traditionally thrown up between technical, business, and artistic people. Performers in the Group do technical and business work, and everyone performs. This theme of mutually supportive work—as opposed to alienating and exploitative labor—was particularly important in doing *Mother Courage*, a play so much about the exploitive distortions of these basic human activities. If Courage becomes a "hyena of the battlefield," the performers telling her story attempt to build a better system of work for the audience to experience. We want the dialectical process built into our work. We want our audiences to experience the contradictions between "story" and "telling the story." We want, and belive we can have, a better world.

I think another important thing will happen. Design is still trapped by scene painting because you spend so much time doing renderings and drawings, because you don't work with real material. So obviously when you finally get down to building a design, you are still visualizing things in two dimensions. But if you start working in a three-dimensional way, even in simple dealings, it will help students become familiar with three dimensions—even four or five dimensions because of the transformations that space can go through. Time is the fourth dimension and the transformations are the fifth.

BMc: Scene designs are rendered from a single vantage point in the audience. When you get into an environmental situation, that single point simply doesn't exist. It's impossible to deal with the complexities of a three-dimensional environmental space from a single point. Environmental design ought to be taught *in situ*, with the work being done in rooms that are taken apart and put back together, rather than on the drawing board.

MOTHER COURAGE AND HER CHILDREN
By Bertolt Brecht
Translated by Ralph Manheim
Music by Paul Dessau. Musical Director, Alexandra Ivanoff
Additional music by The Performance Group
Directed by Richard Schechner
Environment by Jerry N. Rojo and James Clayburgh
Costumes by Theodora Skipitaris
Opened February 24, 1975

Stephen Borst Recruiting Officer, Chaplain, Lieutenant
James Griffiths Sergeant, Cook, Poldi, Soldier
Joan MacIntosh Mother Courage
Leeny Sack Kattrin Haupt
Timothy Shelton Eilif, Sergeant, Soldier, Peasant Boy
Spalding Gray Swiss Cheese, Soldier, Peasant Man
Elizabeth LeCompte General, Yvette, Peasant Woman
Ron Vawter Ordnance Officer, Townspeople, Drummer
James Clayburgh Soldier, Man with a Patch, Clerk

15 Victims of Duty

The Performing Garage is a space in which an ensemble is permanently at work, transforming the same room again and again for each new production. Often, however, groups work in a number of different spaces, creating temporary transformations for a few weeks or even a few days. *Victims of Duty*, presented in 1967 by the New Orleans Group, a forerunner of The Performance Group, led to temporary transformation of a relatively conventional small proscenium, theatre space for an environmental performance. Using platforms, step units, flats, properties, and furniture belonging to Le Petit Théâtre du Vieux Carré, the designers (Franklin Adams, Paul Epstein, and Richard Schechner, assisted by Jerry Rojo and Edmond Seagrave) constructed an environment which drastically altered a studio theatre-rehearsal room. The room was made into a three-dimensional collage of platforms, scenery, and furniture, created by the performers and designers without any formal plan, accompanied by a related collage of slides, film, and sound.

RS: The New Orleans Group was not an actor's group but a director's group. Adams, Epstein, and I were the New Orleans Group. Our first piece—a Happening called *4/66*—was done in April, 1966. I'd directed a lot prior to this, but almost all of it was on a proscenium. In Provincetown, in 1956 and in 1961, I staged things on thrust and in an arena, but it was mostly orthodox except for my production of Sophocles' *Philoctetes*, which was done once on the beach at Truro and once on the steps of the Chrysler Art Museum in Provincetown.

4/66 was done in Bob Seidenberg's second floor loft—a big, new L-shaped, A-frame room. The peak of the room was perhaps 18' high and at the eaves 8'; the long leg of the "L" was about 30' by 40' and the short leg, maybe 15' by 30'. The short leg fed into the stairway from downstairs. In the studio, we set up

chairs, in various kinds of configurations, and a music rack that Epstein constructed. We played different games and performed different events. These had no story to tell. I think it was the first Happening done in New Orleans. *4/66* was fun, and a popular success. We decided to apply Happening techniques to Ionesco's *Victims of Duty*. Le Petit Théâtre du Vieux Carré offered us a room about 40' by 40' by 12' high. With a small proscenium stage at one end. We built the room up with a series of platforms so that the stage disappeared as a separate part of the space. On the former stage was a TV set (with a closed-circuit system), stairways that led to a blank wall, and a table and couch and cupboards filled with hundreds of cups. In the main space (where the audience would be for a proscenium show) was a dining table, an easy chair and lamp, and many risers. These risers filled the space, making a terrain which we covered with rugs. To one side was a spiral tower of chairs which Jerry built. He'll describe it later. On the other side a pair of large doors opened directly onto the street. The Detective made his entrance from the street. At the back was the door leading to the lobby which had a complicated display including film, tape recordings, collage, and hangings. In some ways the *Victims* environment and staging prefigures what The Performance Group did later in *Makbeth* and *Mother Courage*. All over the walls were slogans and graffiti. This idea came back with *Commune*.

BMc: How did you transform the space?

RS: We wanted to make the space into Choubert's living/dining room. Choubert is a provincial Frenchman who finds himself, for no reason, being investigated by a Detective—a basic Kafka plot. There is a scene where Choubert goes up a stairway and disappears. You hear him running in a room above—and he is actually over the audience in the room above.

There is a scene where he goes to the bottom of the ocean: He dives underneath the platforms (there were lots of trapdoors in the platforms), and he emerges first in one place and then in another—dislodging spectators as he pushes up the traps.

BMc: So Choubert's living/dining room is really spread out over the entire space, and contains the audience as well, while other rooms in the house are in different parts of the theatre building.

RS: Right. And we also used the lobby and street. For his entrance the Detective knocks on the loading dock doors of the theatre. Choubert opens the doors onto the traffic in the French Quarter. The Detective's invited in, and Choubert closes the door. Filmmaker Denis Cipnic shot a short film showing the character Nicholas waking up in the morning, dressing, getting on his motorcycle, driving through the street of New Orleans to Le Petit Théâtre du Vieux Carré. In the film, Nicholas arrives at the theatre late in the afternoon. He parks his motorcycle and goes to sleep, propped against the wall of the theatre. The film blacks out after the motorcycle is parked, and the rider goes to sleep. People in New Orleans know New Orleans—it's not like New York City. All the streets Nicholas rides through are familiar to the audience. When the audience gets to the theatre at 8 pm, there is a motorcycle parked outside, and there is someone sleeping next to it, which isn't too unusual for the French Quarter.

When the film resumes, it's night and the man wakes up, starts his big Harley. At the same time, the actor outside gets up and starts his motorcycle. The film ends with the actor driving through the lobby into the theatre. You hear the motorcycle and Nicholas drives it right into the middle of the theatre merging the film and the performance.

The audience leaves *Victims*. During the
play the lobby has been transformed
into an obstacle course. Photo: Matt
Herron, Black Star

BMc: How was the space shared by actors and spectators?

RS: When the spectators arrived in the lobby, they saw a display which filled the whole space—the lobby was about 15' by 30' by 12'. We displayed baby pictures, high school transcripts, resumes, graded college papers, medical reports—hundreds of documents and momentos. There were at least 1000 pictures of people in the production. Whole walls were plastered with pictures from everybody's past. The play is about being investigated. We played a tape recording of the Tulane Naval ROTC Band playing marches, counter-pointed with Hitler's bands playing Nazi marches.

BMc: So when it entered the lobby, the audience was confronted by a collage of different realities.

RS: Right. During the 90 minutes the audience was watching the play, the lobby was transformed. Pictures of Adolf Eichmann suspended from the ceiling, and a huge sheet was strung across the only exit. On it were the words: "I'm a victim of obedience and duty to others," which was Eichmann's statement right before he was executed. As the spectators went out they had to duck under the sheet, and the Eichmann photographs that were hung too low to walk under without ducking.

The play ends with Nicholas repeatedly shouting, "Chew! Swallow!" and stuffing bread down Choubert's throat. We extended that action into the audience, until all the performers were stuffing bread down the spectators' throats—a brutal communion.

When the audience entered, the actors were eating their supper—which really was their supper. Spectators could sit anywhere. Performers greeted spectators they knew, and a few were always invited to sit at the supper table. So there were

spectators at the table, four or five people enmeshed in the center of the play. Then Choubert read an actual item from that night's evening paper about the repressive activity of the government.

Frank Adams was responsible for the scenic organization, Paul Epstein for the sound, I for the action. There were different kinds of electronic music; we needed two technicians to run the sound tapes, closed circuit television, films, and slides. Paul coordinated all that. There was a session where the cast, technicians, Paul, Franklin, and I went into the storeroom of Le Petit Théâtre and blitzkreiged the environment. We threw rugs down, we moved platforms, erected stairs, flung old flats against the walls; we transformed a room with a proscenium into one full space with hills, valleys, passageways, tunnels, and vertical rises. It took about twelve hours to transform the theatre. There were only a few changes after that. We action-painted the environment. It was fun. But the one thing that we lacked was that pile of chairs for a scene when Choubert climbs a pile of chairs reaching to the ceiling. The music for that scene was "Fly Translove Airways Always Gets You There On Time." The scene was kind of an acid trip.

Anyhow, nobody knew how to pile those chairs so an actor could climb them. I knew Jerry Rojo from classes at Tulane. I asked him to come down and solve the chair problem. He did, and we've worked together ever since.

JR: The solution I thought of was to create out of plastic covered steel cable a kind of Christmas tree. The cable was fixed to turnbuckles which could be tightened down, so it had tremendous tension. I used table clamps to fasten the legs of the chairs to the cable, creating a spiral effect with them. The tower was about 12' tall, and probably about 8' in diameter, with

Nicholas, Choubert and Madeleine talk things over near the play's end. Photo: Matt Herron, Black Star

a base of chairs, spiraling upward. There was some sway to the essentially fairly rigid tower.

BMc: To what extent was the blocking and action of the production determined by that twelve-hour blitzkreig?

RS: I really like the principle of action painting. If people work together for a long time, you can face a problem and resolve it in one intense session. you refine it after that. Frank and Paul and I had worked together for nearly two years, and I had worked with the actors and Remi Barclay, the stage manager, for a year. Jerry had known us all for a year. So when we came to the blitzkreig, it was not like getting a group of strangers together. It was not chaotic. We did the same thing with parts of the *Mother Courage* environment. There are no accidents. What appears to be accidental is actually a function of group dynamics. But you've got to work with people who know each other.

BMc: This suggests then that environments begin to function in a production considerably earlier than sets do.

RS: Much earlier. The environment is there, and it has something to say, not so much thematically, but in terms of the basic rehearsal process and group relations. Let's take *The Tooth of Crime*. Jerry says that we met one day and decided to push the things together to make the center structure. When that happened it determined everything else. That decision took ten seconds to make—except it was prepared for by three months work.

BMc: So the environment rehearses too.

RS: Right. The environment is more than the outcome of rehearsal, it is also very much an input into rehearsal. Its like a performer coming in with a characterization different from the one the director imagined. The director doesn't immediately challenge the performer, he wants to see how the new characterization fits in. It's similar for the environment. I believe that's what makes environmental work so much fun; the space is treated creatively like other aspects of the performance, and it can change drastically in a few minutes.

JR: To carry this idea further, it's like living in a house: for a party, you restructure the house; a bedroom becomes a cloakroom; you move the furniture around in the dining room to make a buffet, and so on. You restructure in a particular way because you know your major requirements and the kind of people who are going to be there. But the party itself explores space even more. It deals with it in unexpected ways so that it's a living experience that comes from a set of rules and givens.

The rules of the game for *Victims* called for starting off with a collage of furniture from a traditional theatre stockpile—an interesting notion in itself. We were only going to use stuff from the theatre's prop room and platforms and flat scenery. But it was not used as it ordinarily would be.

BMc: How was it used?

JR: In proscenium theatre, platforms would be used in an illusory way. For example, platforms might be painted to look as though they were made of stone. But here, the platforms simply provided elevation as needed. Somone, Frank Adams, perhaps, would look at the room and say, "That needs to be high over there." That's the origin of the stairs that go nowhere. It's a kind of a building up process—you decide that one corner ought to have a high spot, and it can be like a pyramid seating a lot of people at its base, but with room at the top for only one person.

A view of the environment showing the spiral tower of chairs. The audience has not yet entered. Photo: Matt Herron, Black Star

RS: We took the flats and leaned them against the walls. And then Frank painted graffiti on them. The graffiti texts were lines in the play. The flats also showed images from former productions. *Victims of Duty* is a play about a play. That is also a theme in my work—a lot of plays I do are about the theatre, *The Tooth of Crime* and *The Marilyn Project,* for example. Sometimes I think my life is about theatre, based on theatre; what's basic for me is performing. The *Victims* production cannibalized the stuff of traditional theatre. Cannibalization, incidentally, is central to our work. We don't go out and buy new material or even new actions or images for new environments. We reuse old material. The knife-stab gesture of *Makbeth* was also used in *Commune* and *Tooth.* It's good ecology—and good art. You are your own tradition, and your style gradually develops in a continuity. This is so important in theatre where everything is temporary, evanescent.

BMc: So most of the materials you use have a history, and that history is always present in the environments.

RS: The performers know it, and maybe the audience knows it, too.

JR: You might make an analogy to other artists who work that way. Sometimes people say, "Jerry, your environments seem to look alike," and in a way I guess they do. We use all these 4' by 4' posts—but I think an artist is always working things out, and he goes through a whole series of experiments with shapes and forms and materials.

I was in Avignon in 1973 and I saw a show of Picasso's work. If you look closely, every one of those paintings look alike because they're of a whole body of work.

BMc: The usual premise is that a scene designer is swallowed up in the process of creating a design. Each design is supposed to be uniquely fitted to a play, and the designer, in a sense, disappears. You're saying that, like a painter, your hand is clearly there. This dovetails with something else: you acknowledge the materials you use as materials, and you don't theatricalize them into something else. You use flats as an efficient and interesting way to cover walls; you acknowledge the fact that it's flattage; you don't attempt to transform the flats into something else.

RS: The orthodox theatre uses illusion to create something that apparently is what it is not. We play with the things we have, arrange and rearrange them; we use them to chart our own personal changes. This is what artists always do. Artists are always concerned about the relationships between themselves, their experience, and the world. I think it's hypocritical—or, if not hypocritical, at least destructive of the creative process— for theatre artists to be in the service of other artists, the playwright, for example, or of an abstraction that swallows each of the participating artists. The environmentalist, the performer, the director, the writer, the technician, works out his or her own situation in relation to the experience, the space, the audience, the other people. The experience is not only the experience of the play but the experience of each other. This is true of any genuine ensemble, environmental or not. It was true of the Moscow Art Theatre and The Berliner Ensemble; it is true of the Mabou Mines and the work of Richard Foreman and Robert Wilson.

BMc: An orthodox designer in our own time inherits the realists' distaste for anachronism. Some traditional anachronisms are allowed in conventional settings, but you don't break the rules as they're broken in environmental theatre. In most contemporary theatre, even so-called abstract

A wide-angle view of the environment just before the audience enters. Spectators may sit anywhere. Photo: Matt Herron, Black Star

design is subtractive because you start out from a realist base and take things away. But the realist base is always there. In environmental design, the realist base is not there.

RS: The event itself is there, which is realism in a very different sense.

BMc: There was considerable aggression toward the audience in *Victims of Duty*. Much of that aggression, however, has dissipated over the years. Does this mean you're mellowing?

RS: I think it's not so much a question of mellowing as it is of exploring different relationships with the audience. The aggression has been transformed into ways of collaborating with and manipulating the audience. The first audience contact was that very brutal "Chew! Swallow!" In *Dionysus*, the contact was seductive; in *Makbeth*, there wasn't much contact; in *Commune* it was manipulative and cruel, but it wasn't physically forceful. In *The Tooth of Crime* it's like digging a channel in the beach and letting the water flow down it. The audience doesn't *have* to do anything, but it's pretty hard to resist. In *Courage*, the theatrical event is nested in a social one—the supper—which is a communion shared with the audience.

JR: *Victims* had a violent tone, the audience was stepped on and pushed. I remember, for example, what we called the "interrogation chair." There was almost always a member of the audience sitting in the chair. When the interrogation scene came up, the audience member was forcefully removed.

RS: I think it's not only a change in me, but a change in the performers I work with. As we developed a truly collective group, aggressive energies got worked out within the group

rather than getting thrown against the audience.

BMc: Isn't it also a kind of microcosm for a larger change in the nature of our society? When you and the Living Theatre were working most aggressively with audience, it was a period of shake-ups within the universities, and with youth, a time of open hostility to the establishment and the military. Now we're in a more benign period.

RS: Well, I wouldn't call it benign. It's malignant but squashed down. The resistance we acted out didn't bring the effects we wanted them to bring. I think there will be outbursts again, and soon. I look at myself as a piece of litmus paper: as an artist I'm satisfied with being revealing—showing what is— rather than being innovative. That's not wholly true, but it is a tendency in my work. All I can say is at this moment I am interested in exploring ways of bringing in the audience in more collaborative and friendly ways than before. When the Garage door opens at the end of scene 8 of *Mother Courage*— and it's freezing cold, and the world feels run down, almost stopped, but the war goes on; war and death will be the final activity of our species—is that hostile, a war against ourselves and the audience? I feel a deep and maybe permanent winter is upon us.

BMc: How was light used in *Victims* in contrast to later works?

JR: There was a lot of multimedia slide and film work, so that the theatre, consequently, went dark many times.

RS: Multimedia has dropped out of my work because it's very expensive, and there are other things I want to concentrate on. Also it's better to feed people then spend money on equipment and processing. That was one reason. In addition, there were so many people doing it so plushly in New York, I

didn't feel like competing. And somewhere I sense technology
is not my friend but my bitterest enemy. Death and technology
are pals.

What interests me now is not the use of media but the
exploration of the impulses that bring media into being.

JR: I was looking at some slides of the Czechoslovakian
scenographer Josef Svoboda's work, and it's a case in point.
Because he is in a state-subsidized theatre situation, he is able
to spend as much money as he wants on research to develop
new applications for laser beams and mirrors, hydraulic lifts
and aerosol cans, so that his design is totally technological. He is
really an artist in every sense of the word, because he is taking
theatre into the space age. That's why his work is so powerful.
But there is a general criticism that his work often makes the
living performer subservient to this theatrical space age. Now
that might really be the case. We may be subservient to a
technological world. But I believe there is nothing more
precious then human beings interacting in a simple room with
all its dimensions visible, a space that you can more or less
control with a minimum of light and a minimum of structure. I
think if you come to grips with that you come to grips with a
sense of what humanity is all about. I think a point of view about
life has to be taken.

BMc: Svoboda was the guru of the mixed-media period.
What he created were masques. His was a "rich theatre"
design. But there's no action without reaction and the period
which follows is one of "poor theatre" designing. Many of the
more recent ideas about letting materials be what they really
are, of focusing down on the performer in a simple setting are a
response to the elaborate masques of the Svoboda-dominated
period. This response defines to a considerable degree much of
your work.

16 Endgame

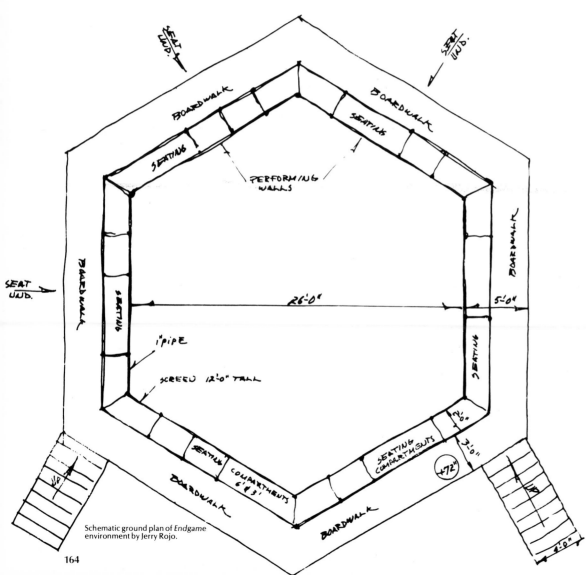

Schematic ground plan of *Endgame*
environment by Jerry Rojo.

For a production of Samuel Beckett's *Endgame,* directed by Andre Gregory and performed by Gregory's Manhattan Project at New York University's School of the Arts, Jerry Rojo, assisted by technical director Marty Kapell, created a hexagonal pavilion with a playing space in the center—28′ in diameter. The playing space was completely encircled by two levels of audience seating, each level broken up into a number of small individual cubicles for spectators. The audience area in turn was encircled by a walkway providing access to the cubicles. Separating the spectators from the performers was a wall of chicken wire and ordinary household screening; when light was directed on to this "wall" from above much like a front-lit scrim, spectators in any one cubicle were virtually invisible from the performance area and from other cubicles.

BMc: When did you begin the *Endgame* Project?

JR: We got into it in December of 1972, and it opened in February of 1973.

BMc: In what kind of space was the environment set up?

JR: The space was formerly a ballroom, in what had once been a catering establishment. It now belongs to the School of the Arts at NYU. The ballroom was divided into two open space theatres, and the one we used was about 40′ wide by 60′ long by 12′ high. It had basic electrical outlets for the theatre and black drapes to mask the windows.

BMc: What did the Manhattan Project want initially?

JR: I got into that project after Eugene Lee—he was their scenic designer for *Alice in Wonderland*—had come up with a couple of solutions to the problem. The one I saw was a tin house of corrugated metal.

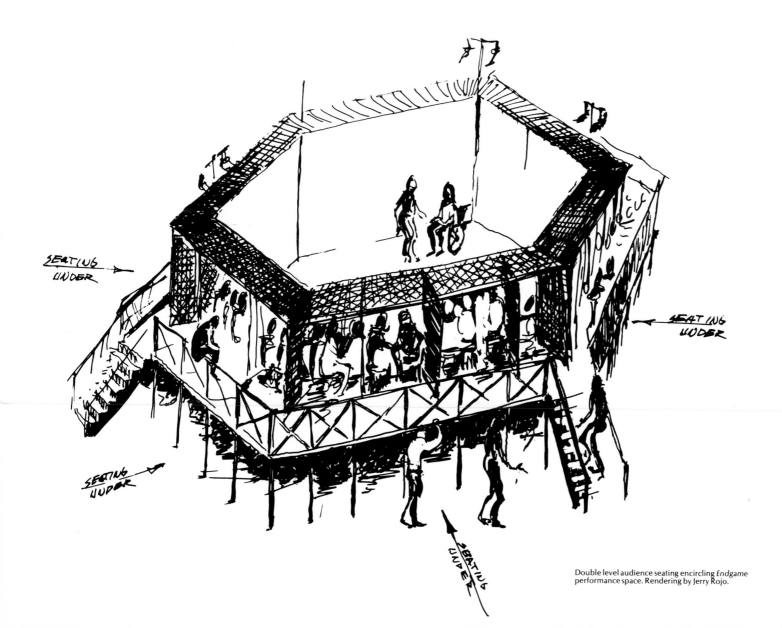

SEATING UNDER

SEATING UNDER

SEATING UNDER

SEATING UNDER

Double level audience seating encircling *Endgame*
performance space. Rendering by Jerry Rojo.

BMc: Would you explain that? What did he do and where?

JR: He built a 25' by 40' room within the room. The ballroom has a 1920's motif and within it he built a small corrugated tin theatre. It was an interesting solution.

BMc: Were both audience and actors inside this theatre?

JR: Yes, so you went into the tin house, which had a roof and four sides. At one end was the stage. The audience sat on ordinary tiered risers on folding chairs.

BMc: Why was it discarded?

JR: They wanted something more environmental.

BMc: What limitations did they place on you?

JR: None at the beginning. They just said, "Come and think about how you want to approach the problem." After seeing the production I felt they were just redoing the traditional frontal approach. I began going at the problem from within Beckett's play, trying to discover what the play wanted environmentally. What I came up with was the idea of setting the audience in the same kind of environmental situation the performers were in, a situation which was very isolated. Part of the idea came to me as I was riding a Greyhound Bus back to Connecticut. As we drove through New York City, I saw that typical New York kind of playground with the cyclone fence around it. And people were standing up against the fence watching like voyeurs. That was an interesting idea so I worked with it. I thought somehow the audience needed to be isolated from the performance, because I felt that the audience wants to understand but does not want to participate in the scabrous goings-on that take place in *Endgame*.
The solution was ultimately a transformation based on two

ideas. One had to do with the cyclone fencing, and the other with the idea of a circle. What developed was the scrim concept of throwing light on the fencing so that you could see out but not in.

BMc: Describe the environment in more detail.

JR: As you come into the space there is a booth at one end where coffee is sold. There is a lot of repetition in the play and we thought that people might want to step out and have a doughnut and then come back, literally take a break from the production. And people did that.

RS: I enjoyed the play a great deal, although I slept through part of it. I like the idea of being able to sleep without insulting the actors. I should add that sometimes I sleep during workshops and rehearsals, and I feel that it's not an insult but a recognition of the autonomy of the event.

JR: The performers were uptight about this, however. There was a tremendous amount of animosity toward them by the audience. People were walking out and going to sleep. In fact, this was the stuff that this performance is made of: little scabrous things going on onstage. The tone of the performance was not very palatable to audiences, so when I presented the actors with the concept of isolation, they liked it. At one time, we even had the notion of using a tank-like structure, a large cylinder with viewing slots in it. The audience would watch through slots, the actors would just see their eyes. But Andre rejected that.

RS: What is rejected is used in the 25¢ nudie peep shows on 42nd Street.

JR: We started with a collection of doors taken from construction sites. They set the tone for the space.

The audience's view of the playing area and audience seating beyond. Photo: Babette Mangolte.

BMc: Where were the doors?

JR: On all the wall surfaces. Then, as you turn to the right, there are two sets of stairs that allow you to go up into the environment proper, where the audience is on two levels. This environment is rather like a two-story, merry-go-round, or a rotunda, that completely surrounds the performing area. The spectators on the lower level can't stand totally erect, although people on the second level can.

BMc: Is this a complete circle—a doughnut—on two levels, broken into cubicles?

JR: Actually there are circles within circles, because there is a companionway all the way around the outside of the circle of cubicles. The cubicles, by the way, hold either two or four spectators.

BMc: On the average what was the size of these cubicles?

JR: The big ones are 6' wide, I think, the small ones about four, so they contain either two or four chairs. The divisions between these cubicles are made of wire mesh above a partial wall, rather like a box stall.

BMc: Could you see from the cubicle to the next?

JR: Yes. Initially we wanted to have a total separation between them, but we discovered that because of the curve you couldn't see much anyway; if you looked to the right or left there were two or three people visible. Beyond them you would be looking around the curve at a wall of wire mesh so you couldn't see the rest of the spectators. We experimented with several kinds of wire. We settled on turkey wire—an ⅛" diameter wire available in different mesh sized—one, two, and three inch. We wanted that particular gauge of wire, but the

openings were too wide to create a scrim effect, so we layered-on ordinary household screening. It was that screening that created the real light barrier. It was so fine that close up you could see right through it, but the arena appeared to be surrounded by a circular wall of light.

BMc: Describe the arena.

JR: It was actually a hexagon, created not so much out of any mystical notion, but from the need to accommodate a certain number of people. The environment could hold more than 100, depending upon whether there were people standing also.

BMc: How was the arena finished?

JR: It was a framed plywood floor covered with aluminum sheets to give it a metallic, hard, reflection quality. There is only one way into the arena, through a door that only the performers use. There is only one because I felt that a sense of incarceration was an important element.

BMc: As you sat in a cubicle, what could you see of spectators directly across from you?

JR: There is a kind of murky quality as you look across the playing area. It is unlike an ordinary arena theatre. Only at a few places are you able to see faces distinctly; they are mostly just vague shapes. This is accomplished through the use of a small floodlights on each of the six sides which is focused partly on the screen and partly on the performing area, so that the entire inside of the arena is very bright.

BMc: What other materials did you use?

JR: Mostly, the companionway was done in 2" by 6" planks or

2" by 4" frames. The attempt was to give the feeling of the platform of a carousel at a carnival. The planks were costly, but we felt they were necessary for the right tone and feel.

All these environments present engineering problems. Here, there was some question as to whether or not the structure would be strong enough. But the kind of framing I developed was self-bracing finally. We didn't really know it in the beginning. I suppose an architect or engineer would have discovered that right away—but I was shooting from the hip. I felt that the structure would lock together properly, and indeed it did.

RS: There were two unsual aspects of the environment that contributed mightily to the performance. The metal floor reminded me of an amusement park electric bumper-car ride. Fun but dangerous. I also thought of frying pans, the cutting room floor, and electric chairs. The room is the kind of space we talk about often but rarely build—a room in which the performers are really isolated from the audience by a fence. The Living Theatre's production of Kenneth Brown's *The Brig* did it a little bit, I suppose, but then the audience was out in front. Grotowski's *Constant Prince* did it to some degree, too. But in *Endgame* there were two really separate worlds, two spheres rubbing against each other. You can't see the audience from the performance space, so the spectators are free to move and change their perspective. I'm sorry there were chairs set up in the passageway because that inhibited audience movement. I think movement should have been encouraged more, that there should actually have been signs out front saying an "endgame" is going on and you can look at it, examine it, walk around it, and study it. The space encouraged that kind of dispassionate, distanced observation. It would have worked for that particular play, and the style of performance, with its pauses and inward focusing.

JR: There was a lot of discussion about just that problem. I think it had something to do with the actors believing audiences would leave the performance. They were prepared to have people walk out. What they were doing was not radical, but was a throwaway, a kind of disposable theatre. The original idea was that the audience could see as much or as little as they wanted, and leave without the actors knowing they had left. That never really worked out because of the intimacy of the space—the least bit of noise was obvious and the audience did not leave. We ended up not encouraging them to leave because of the distraction. Even though it didn't work as we originally planned, from a design point of view it was successful for me because here was a design in which the entire theatre was integral to the context of the play—the theatre was of the play. Any good set does the same thing—it evokes a feeling of the play—but rather than being something that the audience observes as in proscenium or thrust stage design, the design was something the audience occupied. And, incidently, the design won the Drama Desk award in 1973.

ENDGAME

By Samuel Beckett
Directed by Andre Gregory
Environment by Jerry N. Rojo
Opened February 1973

Gerry Bamman Hamm
Larry Pine Clov
Saskia Noordhoek Hegt Nell
Tom Costello Nagg

17 The Great Hoss Pistol

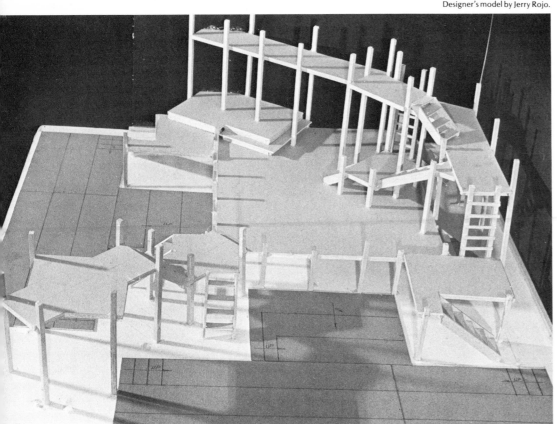

Designer's model by Jerry Rojo.

For the same NYU-affiliated theatre festival at which *Endgame* was presented, Jerry Rojo, assisted by technical director Marty Kapell, designed an environment for *The Great Hoss Pistol*, presented by Section 10, a New York theatre group directed by Omar Shapli, assisted by Andrea Balis. For *The Great Hoss Pistol*, a ballroom in the School of the Arts at New York University was converted to an open space theatre through the use of already existing modular seating units in combination with an environment of platforms and stairs. The environment, used solely by the performers, penetrated the audience seating areas.

JR: Section 10, an improvisational group, is made up of seven performers working out of the NYU School of the Arts.

BMc: In what kind of space did you set up the environment?

JR: The production was part of a festival sponsored by New York University. Two of The Manhattan Project's productions were involved: *Endgame* and *Alice in Wonderland*, and the Section 10 production, directed by Omar Shapli, along with Shaliko Company and the NYU Dance Ensemble. The idea of the festival was that they were all to be in rooms in the same building, the School of the Arts building on Second Avenue. Section 10's production was done in the fifth-floor theatre, a room 100' long by 60' wide, and 22' high. It's an open-space, black box theatre.

BMc: How is it set up?

JR: Jules Fisher designed about eight, tiered, modular seating units for the room. Each unit is independent so you can use it alone and still have a proper stairwell and aisle spacing, and a reasonable number of seats per row. Every unit seats maybe 30 people. Each can be combined with other units to form

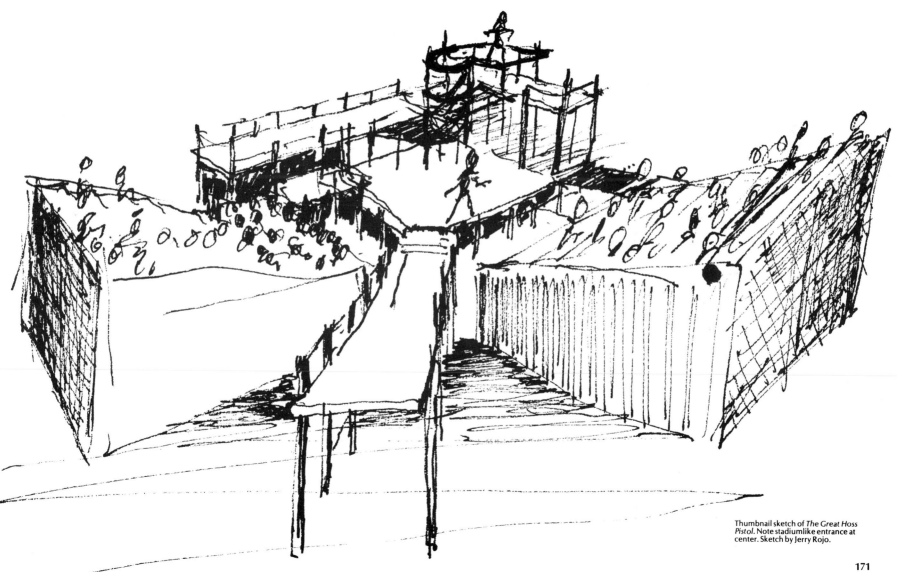

Thumbnail sketch of *The Great Hoss Pistol*. Note stadiumlike entrance at center. Sketch by Jerry Rojo.

Rehearsal of *The Great Hoss Pistol*. Omar Shapli with cast.
Costumes take on aspects of the period yet allow for physicalization.

groupings. The room can be used as an end-stage, thrust, or an arena.

BMc: How did you transform this space?

JR: I couldn't get rid of the seating units because they were so massive, and I thought it would be a challenge to try to make some new kind of use of them. I take particular delight in going into a space and finding a new use for it. I felt that an integral design would make use of these units. There was also the fact that the Section 10 company was not really interested in environmental theatre, in the sense of relating to the audience in new ways. The relationship of the audience to their work is basically frontal. They were more interested in using a complex performer space than in sharing that space with the audience. I felt that I could suggest some kind of arrangement that would expand their concepts about space but still use the modular seating units. I'd seen their previous production, *The Monster Show,* and in it there were some penetrations into the audience area. I felt that the space for *Great Hoss Pistol* might take that penetration even further.

BMc: What did you do with space?

JR: As in *Endgame,* I felt a reluctance to touch the walls of the theatre. I wanted to build another autonomous theatre within the theatre, to construct a totally separate chamber.

BMc: This is essentially the principle that you used in the Inner Auditorium at UConn, isn't it?

JR: Right. Although here, the compounding problem was that *Alice in Wonderland* was entitled to half of the room. They didn't want to use the rolling seating units because the *Alice* environment depends upon their own bleacher units. Section 10 was interested in the modules, however, because they wanted tiered seating. So we used all the units in our half and incorporated them into the total design.

BMc: Describe the route of a spectator.

JR: He enters under the bridge (also a playing area) which is a 15' long walkway, and at the end of it, just before it terminates at the actual area, he turns right or left and goes up into the seating units. The effect was similar to a football stadium, with a pair of grandstands on two sides of the performing area. The stage itself was square with a kind of point, leading into the bridge. The opposite side became a facade behind the performing area, similar to an Elizabethan stage. It was a jungle-jim unit used by the performers, but not by the audience.

This so-called facade was a platform with stairs leading up to different levels. I guess it was roughly similar to an Elizabethan public theatre, because it had "inner-belows" and "inner-aboves" as well as walkways that actors could use above the main performing area. In addition, there were two side areas that penetrated the audience areas on the far right and left near the facade. These areas became intermediate minor stages, 8' square, overlapping the audience and the main stage area, but on a higher level, so that there was clearly a separation.

BMc: How did the production use this environment?

JR: *Hoss Pistol* is a pastiche of scenes about the Revolutionary War period, centering on the Hamilton-Burr conflict. It shows America going from an isolationist period to an imperialistic one. It is a very free-flowing non-linear play with less of a sense of scenes as such, than of a collection of images. The effect is of historical flashbacks, dealing both with archetypal and uniquely American situations. The scenes or images are spread out over the entire environment, although some are rather

specifically localized. For example, Burr's headquarters were set up in the same spot for the entire play. There are two ways to work in environmental theatre; one way is to set the space up so that at any given time all of it is used for all scenes. A second way is to give identity to a particular space for a time and then move to another as the location demands a sort of moving proscenium arch. Section 10 chose, for the most part, to identify spaces within the total environment. This environment did not attempt to relate metaphorically to the play as was the case with *Endgame*. Here, the audience was not integral to the concept of the production. This kind of environment is similar to the Elizabethan theatre, in that there is a separation of audience and performer space; the audience views from a fixed position and the performers use a formalistic or standardized playing area.

GREAT HOSS PISTOL

Conceived by Omar Shapli
By many Americans, Section 10 and Omar Shapli
Directed by Andrea Balis and Omar Shapli
Environment by Jerry N. Rojo
Costumes by Theodora Skipitaris
Music by Warren Swenson
Opened Spring 1973

Abigail Costello Esther Burr and other Americans
Stephannie Howard Sally Hemming and other
Americans
Cecil MacKinnon Theodosia Burr and other
Americans
Stephen Hymes Aaron Burr and other Americans
Ron Van Lieu Thomas Jefferson and other Americans
Charles Pegues Benjamin Banneker and other
Americans
Lee De Ross Alexander Hamilton and other
Americans

18 Ghosts

Environment for *Ghosts*. Photo: Nathaniel Tileston

The Shaliko Company's production of Ibsen's *Ghosts*, directed by Leo Shapiro, opened in April of 1975. With Joseph Papp serving as producer, the production occupied a small room that had originally been a movie theatre, located within the walls of the New York Public Theatre. Designer Jerry Rojo created an environment of lush Victoriana, where the audience pockets function as walls separating the rooms of this Victorian environment. Extending the concepts of environmental lighting, the production is lighted entirely by practical fixtures of the 1910 period. They are integral to the environmental design and controlled by the actors.

BMc: How did the play develop? Did you always know that the production was going to be in this particular theatre in the Public Theatre complex?

JR: No. Originally Leo Shapiro, the Shaliko artistic director, wanted to go into a bigger space. He thought it would be more prestigious, and the upstairs Martinson Hall has a nice Victorian feeling about it which we could have exploited for our production. In the beginning we were working with suggesting spacial and material metaphors. I thought of using framing devices. The audience would see through the frames—quite literally because they would be sitting right in front of them. At the same time the audience would see the actors in the play within frames. And there were to be family portraits adding humor to the events. This idea developed out of the Victorian mansion that seems to put people in compartments—there is always a feeling of ghosts and skeletons in the closets. The frames would have produced a feeling of alienation and it would have seemed more like this production was a little jewel in a museum window. The concept changed when we decided to do *Ghosts* in a more environmental internal way in the smaller, ground floor theatre space—a tiered auditorium about

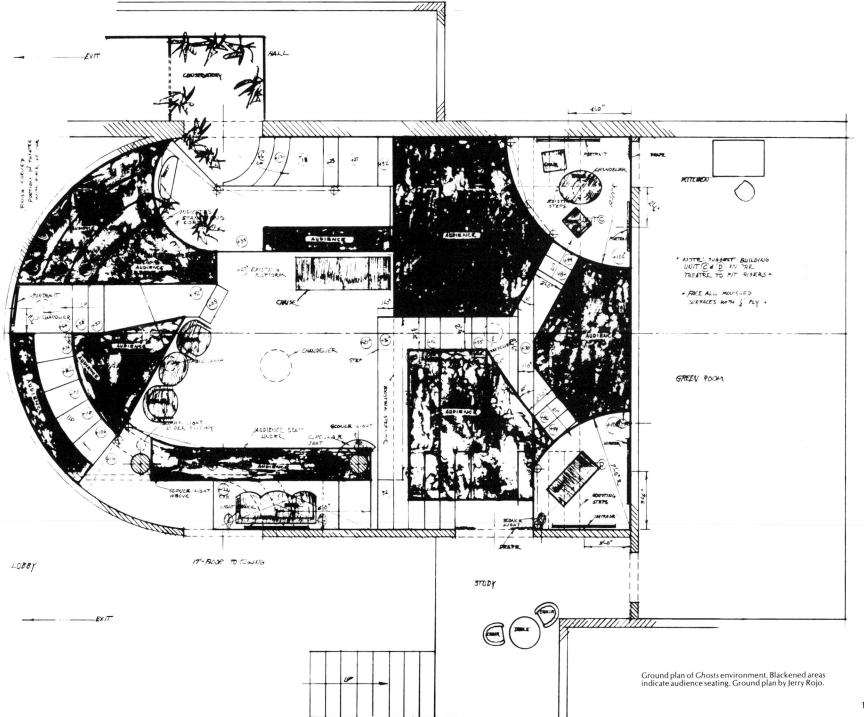

Ground plan of *Ghosts* environment. Blackened areas indicate audience seating. Ground plan by Jerry Rojo.

' GHOSTS '

FOR. SHALIKO

Preliminary sketch for *Ghosts*, not used. Sketch by Jerry Rojo.

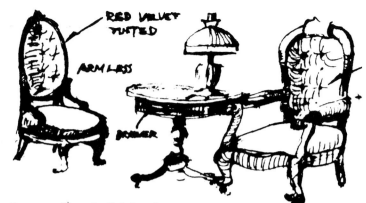

Prop studies by Jerry Rojo.

40' long by 25' wide with a 17' ceiling.

BMc: How did the final design develop?

JR: I think of *Ghosts* as taking place in a Victorian house with lots of rooms, each of them hiding a secret. The soul of the play is that each of the characters has something to hide. I wanted to turn the theatre room into a Victorian house with entrance halls, parlors, sitting rooms, breakfast room, dining rooms, bedrooms, and dressing rooms. Ibsen sets the play in the parlor of the mansion with the greenhouse just behind. He refers to a dining room and an upstairs bedroom. Leo and I decided to use the theatre plus its adjacent rooms. For instance the lobby becomes Mrs. Alving's study. The greenroom has become the dining room. The hallway leading to the Public Theatre's main foyer has become the greenhouse.

BMc: Where does the audience enter?

JR: Just opposite the greenhouse. That door is never used except by the audience. The bedroom was built on a balcony over existing structural columns that were incorporated into the design. In the play much of the action takes place in the parlor but we decided that the action would happen in other parts of the house in such a way that, if the director wanted, he could give the effect that those in the parlor could not hear what was happening in the other rooms.

BMc: How would he do that?

JR: Well, the entire theatre could be used so that everyone could hear everyone; or through staging, the director could suggest that each area is isolated from all the other areas. For example, the bar is definitely isolated from the parlor and from the dining room and the bedroom because between these

areas are pockets of audience. By controlling the lighting, Leo could also designate whether the logic of the entire space was being used—or if the logic of separate spaces was being used. For example, when Pastor Manders is blackmailed about the fire, Engstrand takes him into the kitchen and says, "I'll take the blame for the fire, if you give me the money so I can have my whorehouse." The exchange is just barely heard in the main room. In another instance the bar for Mrs. Alving becomes Pastor Manders' pulpit—Leo understands the ironies of space.

BMc: Is *Ghosts* the first theatre done in the room?

JR: No. Leo, with the Shaliko Company, did Brecht's *The Measures Taken* there in the fall of 1974. The production was severe—a lecture-demonstration. The stage was at the lower end of the room.

BMc: Is all the work Shaliko does severe?

JR: No. The first Shaliko show I was in was *Children of the Gods*, a version of the Agamemnon story. Shapiro had been a student at New York University, he studied with Richard Schechner and was influenced by Grotowski. I was impressed by *Children of the Gods* because I had not yet seen any American production comparable to its physical work—where the body became a fighting machine. The seeds of Shaliko's style are in physical work. For *Ghosts*, Leo has been able to get into it and deal with it on an expressionistic level. When I say expressionistic, I mean actors who really use their own private worlds as catalysts for the roles.

BMc: Has the company been working together long?

JR: Three of them go back to *Children of the Gods* in 1972.

BMc: Have they done anything environmental before?

Pastor Manders and Mrs. Alving in the garden area. Photo: Nathaniel Tileston

JR: *Children of the Gods*.

BMc: Where and how was it done?

JR: At NYU School of the Arts. The performance involved a lot of tumbling, so they covered the floor with rubber mats—made a terrain out of them. *The Measures Taken* was done in a classroom situation. That was why Leo did not want to use the same theatre room for *Ghosts* because he thought of it as the Brecht room. But I thought it would make a very nice room for Mrs. Alving.

BMc: How so?

JR: *Ghosts* is a very sexual play. Oswald returns to Mommy's womb. Mrs. Alving is hot for Pastor Manders. Oswald kisses Regina. In dealing with the subtext, the play says that Mrs. Alving had to sit up nights and drink with her husband so the Shaliko production made her an alcoholic. Also, the relationship between Mrs. Alving and Pastor Manders is probed to a greater sexual depth—as well as her sexual relationship to her son. The room had a shape we could exploit. There is a soft round, womblike end—and the floor and walls are covered with carpeting and fabric.

BMc: What about the use of other materials in the production?

JR: There is an elegant use of soft material for the floors and the costumes. Everyone is involved in a sexual way. The softness of the material is important. The furniture itself is plush and womblike. The furniture gives a sense of a museum to the production—a sexual museum.

BMc: Did you find your furniture or did you build it?

JR: Mostly found it. Jim Carrington, one of the actors in the

178

company, has a good eye for furniture. I did a series of detailed sketches for the furniture and then Jim went out hunting for them.

BMc: How many people does the theatre seat?

JR: 80 to 85. One of the most important elements for me is that the lighting was all practical. Each bit of furniture had a lighting fixture nearby. The room was tied together with authentic furniture and lighting fixtures. The actors had control of the lighting. My concept of environmental lighting is that it should be done from within the production rather than from outside.

BMc: *Ghosts* is different from the other works and projects we have been discussing. Nothing at The Performing Garage uses furniture—except for the green room in *Mother Courage*.

JR: The use of furniture in environmental theatre is different than in traditional theatre where furniture is often decorative. Here Leo uses the furniture as staging areas. The actors put their feet on it. Jump on it. They confront the furniture of the Victorian period. Their rejection of Victorian morality is shown in the treatment of the furniture. Anything can be used by an actor to expand his performance. I look at it this way: the actor's front line is himself. His second line is his costume. His third line is props. The fourth line is the furniture. In some cases, the architecture itself is used. A good environmental actor is highly conscious of all those levels. And in any production the order of priority and importance may be changed.

BMc: Is *Ghosts* lighted entirely from the practicals?

JR: We took the grid out because it gave an undesirable metallic look that defeated the womb concept. There are a

Mrs. Alving and Oswald in living room area with audience seated in close proximity. Photo: Nathaniel Tileston

SCONCE FOR COLUMN

couple of overhead practicals controlled by wall switches—just like in a normal room.

BMc: Is there the impression of light coming from the greenhouse?

JR: Yes, that is one of Leo's ideas. From the greenhouse streams an incredible white light which filters through a lattice and is broken up by plants. The light gives the illusion of a furnace. The intensity of that whiteness is a metaphor of irony and hope. Oswald complains that it is always raining and drab. But the play ends in a blaze of white. Is it hope? The light comes up to full when Oswald is dying.

BMc: Have you ever worked in The Performance Group with practical lighting?

JR: The closest was *The Tooth of Crime*, where the lighting was hot television lighting.

BMc: But wasn't that still lighting from without?

JR: No, because the poles and chandeliers brought instruments to within 6" of the performers. Lighting from without relates to traditional theatre where you don't see where the light is coming from or what it is doing. Those instruments create some "effect." In lighting from within you see what the instruments are doing. They create a specific lighting which the actor relates to. In *Ghosts*, where all the lights are practicals, lighting from within is taken to its extremes. The audience sees the performance and itself in relationship to the lighting. People who are close to the practical see one thing. People who are far away, see something else. In orthodox theatre, lighting would give a more illusionistic feeling. The audience would be out of the lighting and the scene bathed in it.

BMc: How do you deal with a theatre that has an exposed grid?

JR: I don't hide the lighting, but others do. I saw *The Iceman Cometh* at the Circle in the Square in the 1973-74 season—a very realistic play, done with a realistic setting. One of the effects was the change from night to day. You actually saw the instruments but you were expected to go into some never-never land by pretending that the instruments weren't there. Even though the lights were visible, the audience was expected to forget their presence and be conscious only of the effects.

BMc: How does that differ from *Tooth*?

JR: The performers literally used the heat of those lights. The lights were brought into the performance as lights. The audience saw scenes where lighting literally attacked the performers as in a boxing ring. In *Endgame*, I used lighting as a real barrier, shutting the performers off from the audience. There, lighting was used functionally. It can be used to irritate the eyes, to darken the place—not to create an illusion, but to stimulate a direct response.

BMc: From either the actor or the audience?

JR: Especially the actors. The actor is trained to develop associations with lights. For example, when I directed *Baal-Games*, Ekart was played by a tall, blond, light-skinned actor. He associated himself with the whiteness of the lights and positioned himself very high up in the environment where the lights bounced off his white skin making him even more resplendent.

BMc: When a company goes into the Public Theatre does Joseph Papp give them financial assistance?

JR: Shaliko had a deal which gave them the room, a certain amount of publicity, but no cash. Once the environmental concept was worked out and we had a model, we went to Papp and he agreed to build all of it excluding the props. So for *Ghosts* the Public Theatre became in effect the co-producer. Papp scrutinizes all the work that goes on. Leo had success with *The Measures Taken*, and Papp liked the idea of having this experimental thing tucked away in the corner. I don't think he would hand over space to just anyone. The Public Theatre has been subsidized with in-kind help—there is a nice sharing back and forth.

BMc: Did you have any difficulties with the fire laws?

JR: The Public Theatre is certainly conscious of fire laws—they have nine theatres. So the minute we submitted this design we were hit with a lot of codes. I always submit a design which I know is going to push the law—so there is always some compromise here and there. But I overshoot because if you are conservative you'll never get anything done.

"BEDROOM"

Props for Mrs. Alving's boudoir. Study by Jerry Rojo.

GHOSTS

By Henrik Ibsen
Directed by Leonardo Shapiro
Environment by Jerry N. Rojo
Costumes by Theodora Skipitaris
Lighting by Leonardo Shapiro
Opened Spring 1975

Mary Zakrzewski Mrs. Alving
Chris McCann Oswald
Jane Mandel Regina
Tom Crawley Pastor Manders
Jerry Mayer Engstrand